YOUR ASSOCIATION SHORTCUT

the definitive guide for
generating customers
through associations

BY

ROBERT SKROB, CPA, CAE

ISBN: 0615778992

ISBN 13: 9780615778990

Library of Congress Control Number: 2013904223
Association Marketing, Inc., Tallahassee, Fla.

FOREWORD

No one on earth has attended more association events across the world than I have. From Fargo and Coeur d'Alene to San Diego, New York, San Francisco, Amman, Minsk, Tokyo, and Tampa, during the past 10 years I've interfaced with 20,000 associations in boardrooms and classrooms. I've had the opportunity to work with associations as diverse as medical and manufacturing to fraternities and chambers of commerce at the local, state, and national levels—including some of the most successful associations on the globe.

By leading sessions, facilitating strategic plans, and conducting operational audits for associations, I've witnessed thousands of companies that have tapped into the power of associations to generate customers for their own businesses. When it works, it's a beautiful partnership that benefits everyone involved.

This book is the official how-to manual for enhancing a company's market share, sales, and positioning through

America's extensive association community. It guides you through the internal processes used by more than 100,000 trade and professional societies.

Associations are an ideal way to enhance the credibility of a product or a service. It doesn't matter what you sell—*but you must package it to be perceived as a unique offer exclusive to association members.*

I've seen highly successful relationships where a for-profit company receives the endorsement of a highly influential nonprofit. For example, think about the toothpaste or the chewing gum that displays the seal of acceptance from the American Dental Association or the TV commercials recommending products and services approved by AARP.

The technique of selling through associations is as old as associations themselves—many of which are celebrating centennial anniversaries. The outcomes can be significant when an association recommends a product:

- Members respect the association's recommendation.
- Members trust the endorsement and expand their buying (for instance, an endorsed liability product might lead to ancillary sales of other insurance coverages).
- Product credibility is strengthened through logo use or a "seal of approval."
- The company gets new customers and sales (from both members and nonmembers of the association).

The Process

Achieving success with an association will require some insider's information. This book guides you through potential potholes and land mines. Step off the path and the hoped-for endorsement is doomed to fail. Follow the steps outlined in this book and your chances of garnering an association's approval are improved.

The process requires an understanding of an association's priorities, decision makers, and timelines. In recent years, various ethics, legal, and accounting aspects have also influenced the path to success.

Robert Skrob, CPA, CAE, is an association professional with 20-plus years of experience and the respected designation of Certified Association Executive by the American Society of Association Executives. Combining his nonprofit knowledge base with his acclaimed for-profit marketing expertise, he is the first to write in detail about marketing through associations.

This book is a complete guide for building relationships with America's association community, including:

- How to find the associations and identify the best ones for your relationship
- Approaching the most influencial decision makers
- The process from start to finish
- Tips to increase success after the endorsement

Association referrals can significantly improve a for-profit company's bottom line. This book provides the details so your company will understand the opportunity and the process for success.

Bob Harris, CAE, teaches association management throughout the United States and internationally, develops boards, facilitates strategic plans, and troubleshoots. You can access his Association Self Audit template system and learn more about his services at www.RCHCAE.com.

TABLE OF CONTENTS

How to Use This Book to Generate a Lot of New Customers

I was the featured keynote speaker at a seminar, and the morning break was coming to an end. Then the coffee ran out. So, instead of coming back into the meeting room to hear my session, dozens of attendees were standing around the empty coffee urn, cups in hand, waiting for java magically to appear. John, the event's promoter, sprang into action, running to the back of the meeting room and through one of those doors labeled "staff only" into the inner recesses of the convention hotel. The first employee he encountered didn't speak English.

John tried to explain there was no coffee, but the guy didn't understand. Then John tried speaking really slowly, "T-h-e c-o-f-f-e-e i-s e-m-p-t-y." As if the guy who couldn't understand English would suddenly understand the words if John dragged them out syllable by syllable. John tried repeating the same thing, over and over again, until he got exasperated, gave up, and had to walk all the way to the hotel's front desk.

I got my session started on time and worked through the coffee distraction. But the lesson was clear: If two people don't speak the same language, they aren't going to communicate.

It's similar between nonprofit associations and the for-profit world. I've witnessed that both want to work together, but neither understands the other. This causes frustration on both sides, robbing everyone of the benefits of working together effectively.

But there are some glowing exceptions. When it works, it works beautifully. Within the association world, the success stories are legendary. Association executives love to find partnerships that work for their associations. Often, however, they aren't familiar with what for-profit companies want and need, and so the plans break down.

I have enjoyed a unique and ecclectic perspective, with one foot firmly planted in the world of associations and the other just as firmly planted in the world of for-profit enterprise. Here is what I have found: Neither world understands the other, and that is what has kept them from communicating.

In 1999, I purchased an association management company that managed 25 associations, each in different industries. About the same time, I discovered direct response marketing as taught by Dan Kennedy. I purchased courses and applied what I learned to the membership, conference, and sponsorship marketing efforts for my client associations. The results were remarkable. Three of the associations grew to represent more than 95 percent of their potential members. As a comparison, most associations hover around 30 percent.

During a time when associations everywhere were being cannibalized by start-up internet companies eager to build market share, my associations thrived. Plus, I learned a lot from those start-ups. In fact, I noticed that many of those start-ups hosted conferences, and my association clients put on conferences. Some of those start-ups had magazines and publications, my association clients had publications. Many of those start-ups sold memberships and provided members-only sites, my association clients had membership sites. The difference? Those internet companies were for-profit, and my clients were not-for-profit. So, I decided to jump into the for-profit world.

I became the world's leading expert in creating for-profit associations, building more than 37 of them in just a few years. These associations were similar to traditional associations, but they were privately owned. The members didn't care who owned the association. And the best part was, when I got a new member, I kept the money. I didn't have to ask a board of directors for a raise.

I became so well known in the for-profit world that I teamed up with Dan Kennedy and his partner at the time, Bill Glazer, to create the Information Marketing Association (IMA). The IMA is an association of for-profit companies that publish home-study products, provide coaching programs, and put on conferences for their members. These companies are very similar to associations, except they are for-profit.

So, what does all this have to do with you and how you can generate new customers?

For the last 20 years, I've worked with nonprofit associations. I understand how they think because I still work with association boards and put on association events, and my company, Membership Services, Inc., provides full management services for nine associations today.

At the same time, I'm a highly paid marketing consultant to for-profit companies, with clients eagerly paying me more than $5,955.00 a day to help them build complex marketing systems for their businesses. I was even the host of a radio talk show, Business Profits Radio, for more than two years, giving me access to real stories provided by real businesses throughout the country. Because of my experience, *Entrepreneur Magazine* asked me to write five books for them, and they published every one. Each is still available in bookstores today.

This book has three purposes:

Purpose #1: To sell you on using readily available and eager-to-help associations to market to, appeal to, and attract your target customers, thereby transforming your sales and your business life

I see it all the time. Marketers with good products, great relationships with their customers, and a huge opportunity, but they are sitting on the sidelines of one of the biggest games in their industry: associations. Or worse, they are spending a ton of money and getting little to show for their efforts.

With more than 1.9 million U.S.-based organizations, nonprofits and associations have a combined payroll exceeding $47 billion a year. Associations are in every state across the country, helping business owners to comply with laws, grow their businesses, and promote their industries.

Associations represent industries as diverse as accountants to zoos and everything in between. They provide courses, put on events, and have membership programs. They have reach and relevance with a large percentage of their target industries. If the industry association considers something important, people in that industry are going to know about it, whether they agree or not.

For a marketer, associations can be a great source of credibility, notoriety, and most importantly, customers. However, associations can be tricky, unless you understand what you are doing.

Associations and the people who run them are unique; their goals and ways of doing things can be extremely different from those of the for-profit companies to which you may be accustomed. It can be a challenge to understand them, to connect, and to work together. But when you do, the possibilities are amazing.

In my dual role as a consultant to the association world while also serving as a marketing consultant to for-profit companies, I've worked with hundreds of companies to help them market their products through associations. For many, I personally approached the right association and negotiated a great deal for everyone involved.

To give you some insight into what I'm proposing, here are some success stories of for-profit marketers partnering with associations:

An industry vendor secures the opportunity to provide dinner for all members on a key evening of the association's annual meeting. This vendor locks out competitors, has access to the decision makers of his important client companies, and is seen as giving back to the industry that supports him. The association gets a fun, free event to attract attendees to its annual meeting.

The author of a home-study course works with the association to provide his introductory course as a welcome gift for all new members. First, all new members receive his product. Second, the association promotes this vendor and his product to all prospective members in the industry as it markets its membership.

A professional speaker creates a course together with an association. The association conducts marketing in communities throughout the country for one-day membership seminars. The association fills the room and pays the speaker to provide the presentation. The speaker gets to sell his products and consulting services at the back of the room during the event, generating revenues the speaker gets to keep. The association gets a membership benefit it couldn't provide without the speaker. The speaker gets a free stream of new customers, plus a ton of free promotion to prospective attendees throughout the country.

A new consultant, on her own for the first time, is a featured speaker at an association's meeting. She immediately moves from "nobody" to "featured expert" in her subject area.

An author gets his book included in the association's bookstore. On Amazon his title gets lost among millions of other books. In the association's bookstore, promoted in the association's publications and at events, his message reaches his most likely prospective customers.

A publisher partners with all the chambers of commerce in its county to publish membership directories and economic development publications, giving this company instant credibility with members and producing seven figures for its book and newspaper publishing companies.

An attorney provides a free "helpline" to answer association members' questions. The service is promoted to members as an association benefit, and, get this, the association pays the attorney to provide this access. The attorney earns a fee plus a steady stream of new client referrals.

A vendor at association trade shows generates solid leads each time he exhibits, and converts them through a follow-up process after each event.

A marketer creates a "turnkey" system for associations, making sure there is zero work required on the part of the association. This has been extremely successful for one company, generating millions of dollars in revenue.

Another marketer works with hundreds of home builder associations, chambers of commerce, and other specialized member-driven associations to increase their memberships by positioning his product as a member benefit that attracts new members to the association. His program increases membership in the association and generates leads, which has created more than $20 million in revenue for his company over the last seven years.

A speaker presents to chambers of commerce throughout Southern California, generating leads and closing more than $100,000.00 in new business.

An entrepreneur is endorsed by eight state associations in one region of the United States, generating 85 percent of his company's gross revenue.

While most independent insurance agents struggle, a small two-person family agency reels in a large six-figure salary as the exclusive provider of insurance for an industry association's membership. By paying the association a consulting fee, this agency receives aggressive promotion to association members. The agents can specialize on the issues and carriers for that industry, doing a great job for members and creating a nice living for themselves.

These are just a few of the success stories I've witnessed within the association world. The most important element in all these stories is the effort was a win for the association because it received a benefit it could provide members, and in some cases, the partnership provided direct revenue for the association as well. And it was a huge win for the for-profit because it received a steady stream of new customers.

> **Purpose #2: To give you a new understanding of what associations are, where to find them, how you can access their members, and how you can get out of your own way and get in sync with an association partner**

Success with associations can be elusive. I've seen hundreds of people fail in their efforts with associations:

- Speakers by the hundreds (and their poor staff members) cold call associations to ask for paid speaking gigs. As if an association would hire a speaker who needs to cold call!
- Companies want to offer associations a membership benefit, but they don't understand that three members of the board of directors have already pitched similar opportunities and the executive director has had enough problems with them already.
- A publisher has his own products to promote, but the tone and language used in his marketing isn't consistent with the image the association is trying to portray. It is like showing up at a black tie dinner wearing jeans and a T-shirt. It may make

that publisher happy, but it's a big failure if the goal is to impress the people wearing black ties.

- An entrepreneur can't sell his product himself, and so he wants to give the association a percentage to do all his marketing work for him. Association leaders are looking for a partner, and a "game" partner at that. Do you think an association executive is going to take a chance on recommending a product when this guy can't sell it himself?

- Oh, and don't forget the industry vendor who wants to offer the association a complimentary service in lieu of paying membership dues and/or a sponsorship. If the association does it for one, it has to do it for everyone else.

The Reason Most Marketers Struggle When Working With Associations

The list above doesn't even get me started on the association marketing horror stories I've witnessed. Most of the marketers' efforts are hapless failures, not because of incompetence, but because they just don't understand how associations work. And worse, even when you explain the differences, they insist on doing what makes sense to them based on their experiences within the for-profit world.

Here are just a few of the recent comments I received when I asked about marketers' experiences when working with associations:

- "Met quite a few people, but the turnaround time on sales is slow."

- "Overall, a relatively high cost with little return. Attendees were there largely to earn continuing education credits and the free beer/snacks, so we would get very little real interest. The association's view was that it would be 'ideal' and charged accordingly. Very limited return for a relatively high outlay."
- "Hard to find the decision maker, or the decision is made by committee—need to sell four or five people on the idea."
- "My experience is that the CEOs, presidents, and business owners who contract for my consulting services are not in the audience. Out of several dozen events, I've been able to follow up and contract once."
- "I've been a vendor at an annual meeting. Got a lot of leads—but didn't have a good system in place at the time to use them effectively."

... and this is just a sample of the hundreds of comments I've heard about how frustrating it can be to work with associations.

For the most part, these marketers aren't failing because of any problem with their product or opportunity. In fact, there are many good ways they could work with an association that would be a win for everyone involved. But because the cultures are so different and the business owner has so little understanding of associations and the ways they operate, the deal fails before it ever gets started.

Some of what you read here is going to feel counterintuitive. That's the point of the book: to give you insights into a perspective you may not have and an experience you don't share, and to help you join a culture that's foreign to you.

Throughout this book I'm going to reveal the easy way you can work with associations to generate customers for your business.

Purpose #3: To present a collection of strategies for successfully marketing through associations and ultimately to put it into the context of a step-by-step system

I've provided training programs for industries as diverse as accountants, dentists, motorcycle dealers, and acupuncturists. This experience, together with extensive study of instructional design, has taught me how to provide training resources that will help you get results quickly.

First we will cover the background information and theory you need to prepare you for working with associations. Then I'll show you a systematic approach to put all this newfound understanding to work for you in the real world. My life's work has been about building marketing systems—and I'm often paid $50,000.00 by clients to do so. For the last 20 years, I have worked with associations, helped companies to create marketing plans, and built marketing systems. You can be assured that the systematic approach I prescribe here will work for you—in any type or size of business, selling any product or service.

But a word of warning: Approaching an association is like visiting a different country. Things look similar except for those big exceptions—like everyone driving on the "wrong" side of the road. When visiting those countries, you've got to break old habits—like looking left for approaching cars so you aren't hit by a car approaching from your right.

This guide is your welcome mat to a different world, full of untapped opportunities and fulfilling ways of doing business, once you get accustomed to them.

This book is not meant to be a lecture; instead, my goal is to start a conversation with you. I have additional resources and information prepared for you at www. YourAssociationShortcut.com. You'll want to join the mailing list. I'll share new case studies and profiles with you as more and more people begin to implement the lucrative Association Shortcut to effective marketing you'll learn about in the pages of this book.

MARKET TO THE MEMBERS, NOT THE ASSOCIATION

I never thought my son would be taking a shop class. Robert is in 8th grade. His schedule was determined by the science and math classes he wanted to take, so he was forced to take an elective for 4th period. Although he would have preferred to take keyboard or some other music class, those weren't offered at that time, so his only choices were shop and PE. Turns out he loves shop. In shop he gets to use four different types of saws, a drill press, and sanders.

For the first four weeks of shop class, Robert's teacher taught the students only how to draw. Even now, before they cut anything, they have to draw what they plan to build from several different perspectives. For instance, if it's a wooden tool caddy, a small box with a handle at the top, Robert has to draw pictures of what the caddy will look like from the top, the bottom, and two different sides. This way, he can demonstrate that he knows what it should look like before he starts cutting.

It's amazing how good Robert has become at building things. At 13 years old, he can cut wood to create beautiful, practical objects. While I'm proud of my son, it's not the magic of the kid; it's the magic of the process.

For several weeks, the shop teacher teaches his students how to create drawings before they touch the saws. Then, as their skill in creating drawings improves, he can introduce the saws and demonstrate how the drawing makes it a lot easier and better when it comes to actually cutting the wood and building the object. Plus, while the drawings allow the students to produce better finished products, what is more important for a school system on a tight supplies budget is that those drawings allow the class to be a lot more efficient with the resources.

Here is my son, Robert, with an Adirondack chair he made in his shop class. It's amazing what you can accomplish when you follow simple instructions outlined by someone who has gone before you.

Now Robert is making cool stuff like Adirondack chairs in shop class; he's working on his second one as I write this book. Much like the shop teacher's required drawings, you and I are going to cover some things that may seem basic, but they are important to ensure we both have the same understanding as we go along. Each concept will get progressively more complex as we proceed.

First, I'd like to clarify something important before we get too far into this book. The purpose of this manual is to give you insight into associations so you can access their members as potential new customers. It is not meant to encourage you to market to the association itself to get *it* to be your customer.

If the association becomes your customer, fine. But the real power of association marketing is to work *through* the association, to use it as a high-speed expressway leading right to a group of ready and willing customers. Customers who are eager to listen to messages created expressly for them, relevant to their daily lives, for products and services that solve their unique problems.

The last part of the preceding paragraph is critical. As you conduct an association marketing program, you need to be marketing "problem solutions." Let me stress it again: I don't care what products or services you are selling, you need to be selling "problem solutions," and there is a very easy way to get started. Make a long list of all the problems each of your products or services solves. Then for each of those problems, create a list of individuals who have those problems. Take a moment and create those lists right now. Use the margin of this book or the bottom the next page.

Your lists will serve as the foundation of your niche-marketing program. Following is the critical information that will allow you to leverage your lists into a super-effective marketing program.

Association Marketing Questions Answered

As soon as word got out that I was writing this book, I received a flood of questions. I also received some success stories, but mostly I heard questions and expressions of frustration from companies that would love to work more closely with associations.

Here are 75 examples of the many questions I received from companies about how to market through associations. I'll answer these questions for you within the pages of this book:

1. How do you win them over?
2. How do I establish partnerships with the associations?
3. How do we become more effective at attracting potential clients into our exhibit booth? How do we catch their attention in the few seconds they are walking by our booth?
4. What is the most effective way to make a return on our investment?
5. How do I build a marketing funnel to associations that can be duplicated and doesn't require my constant presence?
6. How do I create a stream of new leads?
7. What are the best practices for developing a successful process for teaming up?
8. Are nonprofit associations generally open to sharing the profits in a joint venture?

9. How do we structure a "next step" offer within the limitations most associations put on selling during presentations?
10. What is the process of attracting them vs. chasing them?
11. What is the best way to proactively boost the fortunes and profile of the association through our help and support?
12. How do I get associations to take notice of what I have to offer and become joint venture partners?
13. What other associations would be a good fit?
14. What are best practices for gaining an association's endorsement?
15. How can I improve my follow-up?
16. How do we get approval to sell from the stage or at the back of the room?
17. How can I establish such a high level of influence that they will ask me to speak/present at their functions?
18. How can I protect a product or an idea from being "given" to the association's top sponsor instead of working with me?
19. Where do I get a list of associations? How do I approach them?
20. How do you become magnetic and differentiate yourself so the association is prepared to promote you actively to its members?
21. Is there a system for identifying the best people to reach out to, gain their attention, and leverage that into some kind of ongoing partnership (delivering speaking, online education, tools for members)? If so, what is it?

22. How can I build more effective long-term partnerships with the right associations?
23. How do I get to the right person who can influence the decision?
24. How can we work together for maximum mutual benefit to all parties inclusive of the end client?
25. How do I gain the trust of the association's leadership in order to gain access to membership information?
26. What most motivates associations? What do they really want?
27. Do associations want discounts for their members, good speakers, commissions on sales if they do some type of mailing or emailing, a way to get more members (maybe through cross promotion), etc.?
28. Is there a common theme or a "hot button" item that when pitched to association executives gets their attention enough to be interested to hear more?
29. How can we systematize marketing so it's not like reinventing the wheel each time?
30. How can I get past the "we love what you've got, but we can't be seen to favor any particular product or service"?
31. How do we identify what the association wants to be able to pitch to them successfully?
32. How do I find associations, and how do I present myself and my information?
33. What is the best way to get known and be seen, to build trust and a reputation as a professional with specific services to offer?

34. Influencers are great, but where are the decision makers at these events?

35. How can I improve my follow-up and access to decision makers?

36. Why don't associations give me a real shot at promoting my business instead of making it a limited, perfunctory gesture?

37. How do I get to the decision makers?

38. How do you get a large association to make decisions when there are politics and multiple board members with multiple agendas?

39. How can I best focus my "elevator speech" and get decision makers to listen seriously?

40. How can we nail down the win-win revenue generating side of an opportunity BEFORE investing in dues and other participation/access costs?

41. What's your best strategy for pitching a joint venture with an association?

42. How can I make contact with associations in non-art fields, and how can I find out what they might be looking for?

43. How can I find the associations that are willing to pay for professional speakers?

44. How do you create a successful track record with one association so that it opens doors for secondary/ancillary associations?

45. How can I book more association speeches and webinars, and get results from the effort?

46. How do I develop relationships with the executive directors or program directors so that I'm known to them when I offer something to their members?

47. How can we effectively research an association's current activities, organizational structure, and skills?
48. Where do I start, and to whom do I talk to get started?
49. How do you get the group to actively participate in promoting your service?
50. What do they want to see from us?
51. What are key entry points for marketing speaking engagements, books, info products, etc.?
52. How can we scale our company to accommodate more associations and groups?
53. How do you get them to sponsor your services/products?
54. What are the best ways to generate revenue? Is it the exhibit area? Being a speaker? What?
55. How do you leverage it to achieve greater sales?
56. How much time do I need to invest in building and maintaining it?
57. How do I make money doing it?
58. Will they provide a list of members and their email addresses?
59. How can I find more associations looking for experts/content?
60. How do I find the best associations for the target information I have? How do I know which associations have "buyers" and which ones are primarily filled with people who want information only?
61. How can I get in faster and speed up the process?
62. What are the hottest and best ways to get their attention and get action faster?

63. How do you make a pitch that will be accepted at first shot?
64. How and whom should I approach in the beginning?
65. What are the best strategies that work most reliably, including the best offer to get them to provide their contact data, and how do I follow up to get substantial business?
66. How do I establish a reputation as a resource?
67. Why does it always cost so much to connect with them?
68. How do I get in front of more ideal associations (a list would be great!), and how can I automate the process?
69. Which associations should I focus on?
70. How do I get my information out to more associations?
71. Which is the best format to package the information for effective presentation?
72. How can we get joint ventures or access to the membership without doing a trade show?
73. What is the best way to get articles published?
74. How can we get them to actually endorse us?
75. How can we best approach and structure arrangements whereby they get what they need and we get access to their communities to promote our products?

Wow, this is a lot to cover! So, if I answered every single question on this list, would you consider this book a 5-star success?

Some of the answers to these questions could become, by themselves, a full three-day seminar. However, I've stepped up to offer the answers as completely as possible within the pages of an introductory book.

So, since this list is so long, we better get started right away. Read on!

An Introduction to Marketing Efficiency

My wife and I were having dinner in our dining room while the news played on the television in the adjacent living room. Although we weren't paying much attention, one of the teases before a commercial break caught our attention.

"Police shoot dog on Eddie Road! Story right after this."

My wife, Kory, and I looked at each other. *We* were living on Eddie Road. We were accustomed to police stories being about neighborhoods on the other side of town. Now the police were shooting dogs on our street!

It got worse.

The news video showed the house where the shooting occurred—and it was right across the street. Yes, directly across the street from the little yellow house where Kory and I lived with our 2-year-old daughter.

The police came by to arrest a guy who had failed to appear in court. The guy sent his dog after the police. To defend themselves, one of the officers shot the dog and killed it. During the distraction, the perpetrator escaped.

There I sat, living across the street from someone the police had come to arrest, in a terrible neighborhood with my family. I glanced at the swing set in our backyard where I frequently played with my daughter. We needed to move.

My wife and I lived on Eddie Road because we had no choice. We were married young, and Kory was pregnant before our first anniversary. Both of us brought debt into the marriage, and together we owed more than we earned in a year. Plus, my wife didn't go back to work after our daughter was born. She didn't make enough at her job at Home Depot to justify the time and expense. We had to grow up quickly.

All this made us work harder. Kory babysat for one of her friends, generating more than she would have in her job. Plus, we started a new courier business, walking license applications through Tallahassee's government offices in the time before you could apply and renew online. Within a few years, we generated the money we needed and paid off everything we owed, plus interest.

Today we live in a nice home and enjoy spending time by our pool, but I'll always remember where we came from. Those experiences gave us the work ethic we have today.

I wanted to share this story with you so you would know I wasn't born successful; it came from intense study and practice of what I'm sharing with you in the pages of this book. I expect the information you'll learn here will lead to a similar transformation in your business and your life.

There are hundreds of thousands of registered nonprofit associations throughout the United States. These associations represent industries and professions, some worldwide in scope, and others with national, state, and even regional or local distributions. These organizations can be trade organizations representing an industry or businesses, individual membership organizations representing groups of individuals with a common interest, or professional societies representing a particular professional designation or group of professionals. Associations apply for exemptions from income taxes. In the United States, these tax exemptions are known by the Internal Revenue Code statute that grants them. The two most common are 501(c)(6) and 501(c)(3) organizations.

There are approximately 100,000 tax-exempt organizations under 501(c)(6) of the Internal Revenue Code. These organizations include trade associations, businesses, chambers of commerce, and professional associations. To be tax exempt under 501(c)(6), an organization must have the following characteristics: (1) It must be an association of people having a common business interest, or its purposes must be to promote a common business interest; (2) It must be a membership organization; (3) It must be organized as a nonprofit; and (4) No part of its earnings may benefit an individual or a board member.

Charities, foundations, and other donor-based organizations are included within 501(c)(3) of the tax code. There are at least a half-million 501(c)(3) organizations in the United States. These include charities, religious organizations, and nonprofit groups. To meet the requirements of 501(c)(3), an organization must meet the following requirements: (1) It must operate exclusively for one or more of the following purposes: charitable, religious, educational, scientific, literary, testing for public safety, fostering national or international amateur sports competitions, or preventing cruelty to children or animals; (2) None of its earnings may go to a private individual or a board member; and (3) It may not do any "significant" legislative activities, and it may not participate at all in political campaigns.

Notwithstanding item 3 above, associations are often known for their political activities. Many of them make large investments of time and money into communicating their members' needs to lawmakers. The other side of the legislative action coin is the communication of what is happening within the lawmaking process to the association's members. It is a common joke among association leaders that "we protect you from the people you elected."

Lawmakers have come to rely on associations as a resource for specific industry knowledge and the expertise they need when crafting new laws, many of which have a broad impact on all constituents.

While many trade and professional associations conduct extensive political action programs, few associations do legislative and political activities exclusively. Other program areas include:

You can see evidence of associations interacting with your customers on any street corner. Associations serve every profession and industry. Your potential customers are already interacting with their associations by reading emails, poring through magazines, completing home-study courses, and attending seminars.

Education

Over 90 percent of all trade and professional associations have education programming as one of their major program activities. Most associations offer programming as large, national multi-day events, featuring multiple speakers and multiple sessions running concurrently. Often these programs are in conjunction with a trade show or other sales opportunities. Associations may also offer smaller regional meetings with fewer breakouts and speakers, and perhaps held over fewer days, that focus on issues that impact a particular market area. State associations often have programs with multiple speakers and several tracks that focus on statewide issues, and regional and citywide events are also common. Other programs include specialty seminars that feature specific information on one topic. These programs can range from a two-hour program to a two-week specialty course. Many associations offer programs for members new to an industry or a profession so they can gain a broad base of knowledge for their operations. For the most part, associations offer education at a low price that is not available from for-profit businesses.

Certification

Many associations create professional and product standards within their industry and then educate and certify their members on those standards. Members prefer voluntary standards over government regulation because they are more flexible and adaptable to a changing business environment. Many of the credentials you see behind individuals' names or the accreditations achieved by businesses are acquired on a voluntary basis through an association's certification program.

Best Practices

One of the common issues you will hear about at association meetings is those "fly-by-night fringe operators" that operate in an unscrupulous manner. There is nothing more frustrating to businesses than hearing about operators that break the law or break the code of conduct within an industry, especially when they injure consumers. A significant portion of the programming of most associations involves the communication of government regulatory information to aid members' compliance and to create a shortcut members can follow that is not known by non-members. The goal of establishing best practices is to "raise the bar" within the industry while ensuring a level playing field for all competitors and consumers.

Research

Associations and mature industries play a huge role in providing information for businesses and individuals within the industry to operate more effectively. This information usually develops through surveys and other collection devices, and it offers benchmarking opportunities for individuals to see how their businesses are progressing as compared to industry averages. Associations also compile lists of bad debtors or customers that have caused the industry harm in the past. And many times associations will conduct analyses of the industry's needs and develop job descriptions, forms, and other documents that aid members in the efficient operation of their businesses.

Directories/Coaching

Many associations offer employment-related information. If it is an association of employers, the group will very often offer a job bank for job seekers, compliance information on effective employee management, and other tips for employers to aid in the effective recruitment and motivation of employees. If it is an association made up of employees, most often the association's materials will include advice on career advancement and job skills that will help its members advance their careers more efficiently.

Benefit Programs

Associations strive to create "golden handcuff" benefits
that provide an attractive return on investment for
members. For instance, an association may provide access
to an insurance program that saves members so much
money that it makes the cost of membership dues free, or
at least a no-brainer. Or better yet, the group might offer
a benefit that members use with their customers. This
way, the member has to retain his or her membership to
continue the relationship with his or her customers.

In reality, few benefits rise to golden handcuff status.
Most are simple discount programs for products and
services that members frequently buy.

Associations can become an effective tool for any niche
marketer. These organizations and the individuals within
them live and operate within the niche on a daily basis.
The information they have and the contacts to which they
have access are critical resources that could take years
for an individual niche marketer to create on his or her
own. Most niche marketers identify a target market by
slicing and dicing different industry, demographic, and
psychographic information into lists of likely customers.
Association marketing shortcuts that process because
the association has already created an organization of
individuals, all of whom meet the particular industry's
demographic and psychographic criteria. While it may
not have been your first choice as a niche marketer, it is
a huge shortcut to getting real sales and generating real
customers for your business through your marketing
efforts.

There are two main methods of accessing the members of an association to generate new customers. The first option, which we will call *association marketing*, uses all the standard programs an association already provides to its members. This approach allows you to target your advertising and marketing programs, increasing their relevancy and effectiveness within the market you are trying to reach. The second option, *endorsed provider marketing*, requires a strategic relationship with the association. Entering into an endorsed provider relationship allows you to use many of the same association marketing opportunities available to everyone else, but it also gives you the additional advantage of having the "seal of approval" from the association.

Depending on what you are trying to achieve through your niche-marketing program, both association marketing and endorsed provider marketing offer unparalleled opportunities for generating sales and new customers.

Association Marketing

Providing companies like yours with an opportunity to reach their members is an important revenue source for most associations. However, they are extremely cautious about these arrangements because if they allow vendors too much contact, their members can become frustrated and cancel their memberships. When you approach it in the right way, however, this audience can be a lucrative group of customers and new customer prospects for you.

Membership
Over half of all associations offer a membership option for vendors who are interested in participating in the industry association. This membership option is generally called associate or affiliate membership. Associate membership offers vendors increased exposure and visibility within the industry, usually provides these companies with ongoing information and updates about new industry trends and opportunities, as well as grants

the vendor access to the association that is unavailable to non-members.

The most common associate member benefits include subscriptions and discounts for advertising in the association's magazines, advanced notice and discounts on the association's trade shows, and access to participate in education programs. Many associations even allow associate members to serve on the board of directors of the organization.

You should note that associate membership does not in any way include an endorsement of you as a vendor to the industry. However, through your participation in the industry's events and your inclusion in the association's buyer's guide or associate member listings, it will become clear to the association's members that you are a vendor who cares about them as an industry and not just about the next dollar of business. This will go a long way toward building lasting trust and strong relationships with the association's members.

Association Meetings
You should participate in the association's meetings to the extent your schedule allows and your participation makes sense within your marketing plan. Most associations will ask you to sponsor, to exhibit, or to otherwise spend a lot more money than average registrants spend to come to an event. While the education's content may not be completely relevant to you, I suggest that you at least start within an industry by simply attending the event as a registrant. Associations usually offer significant discounts to the registrants of a meeting because they have generated sponsorships that pay a bulk of the event's expenses. This creates a valuable opportunity for you to mingle with the

registrants during the education, during the breaks, while sitting at one of the education tables, and in impromptu settings before the meetings start and certainly after they end. It is also a terrific opportunity to sit with prospects during a luncheon, if one is provided, or to offer to take a couple of industry members to lunch if a meal is not being offered by the meeting's host. There is nothing wrong with getting additional publicity and recognition from being an event's sponsor or exhibitor. However, it may not be worth the price. I have seen a lot of good marketers do very well in a niche by simply attending a meeting and hanging out as "one of the folks." Where else can you interact for a day with 10, 20, 50, 100, or 200 members of your target market and best customer prospects?

Sponsorships

As your familiarity with the industry and the individuals who attend the events and meetings grows, I highly recommend that you consider sponsoring one or more events. One of the most important considerations you should keep in mind (and one of the most common ways I see target marketers fail) is to have an end goal when you sponsor an event. What are you trying to achieve when you spend the money to sponsor a meeting? Name recognition is probably not enough. You should have a dedicated offer or a new product to present or a customer acquisition technique in place to leverage the sponsorship opportunity.

When the meeting's attendees are giddy with appreciation after having enjoyed the event you sponsored, you need to be ready with an offer they cannot refuse, with a product they would love to have that solves a problem that has been nagging them for years. This is a formula for massive ROI on a sponsorship investment. And it is the only formula you should use when sponsoring an association's event.

Conventions/Trade Shows

Many associations offer trade shows. These events provide an important opportunity for you to participate in a showcase of products and services available to an association's membership. Many times, trade show registration for attendees is offered at inexpensive or nominal rates, encouraging vast numbers of attendees to peruse the displays. Your associate membership will put you at a strong advantage over other exhibitors who are looking for access to the trade show. Associate members often get advanced notice of the trade show as well as preferred placement in the exhibit hall. Again, this is an environment where you need to have a specific outcome in mind—and a plan to generate that outcome. Simply standing in your booth, hoping for people to come to you, is not enough.

While "How to Exhibit" could be an entire book of its own, let me give you one tip here; the key to successful exhibiting is to sign up buyers. Develop a system for individuals on the trade show floor to become buyers. On the next page you will see a photo of an exhibit booth I created when I exhibited at the National Speakers Association's trade show. I promoted a $100.00 a month continuity program teaching speakers how to create home-study courses and newsletters. (I owe Tom Orent of Gems Insiders Circle a big thanks because he pioneered much of what I did in his exhibits at dentists' trade shows.)

At my booth I offered a FedEx box full of training materials for $1.00, charged on a credit card with a two-month free trial membership in my continuity program. Over three days, along with the help of one full-time, top-notch assistant, we generated 132 new sign-ups in the program. Then I had the opportunity to keep them as members over the two-month free trial membership period.

Too many vendors exhibit at trade shows with the idea of "getting your name out there." Most should figure out a way to encourage attendees to sign up right there on the exhibit floor. As Dan Kennedy teaches, "Always be selling."

Association Advertising
While many associations are rushing to put their member communications online, either via email blast or through websites, most associations still have a printed newsletter. All of these communication media offer opportunities for you to connect with your target industry.

Many of these online and offline publications offer advertising opportunities. These advertising opportunities often go overlooked because few associations have professional sales teams dedicated to promoting them. However, association publications score very well in readership surveys and have a strong trust relationship with their members. While the circulation could be much higher, the advertiser benefits from the high readership that associations' publications enjoy.

Also, be aware of the opportunities for getting free publicity for your company and its products and services. Associations routinely make announcements about new products, new services, or other news that may be of interest to their members. In addition, associations are often looking for content for their newsletters in the form of articles that show members how to solve their problems.

Mailing Lists
While this is not as popular as it was 10 years ago, many associations still offer their mailing lists for sale or rent to associate members. Often these are available in the form of labels ready to go on your mailing, or you can obtain the same information through printed or online membership directories that associations offer their members. These lists provide huge opportunities for the target marketer to conduct campaigns directly to the individual members of an association. Because each member has a financial relationship with the association, the association is communicating with each member at least annually, but probably 10 to 15 times a year. This volume of mail ensures that the association's mailing list is one of the most accurate representations of the industry.

Marketing Through Associations Became the De Facto Choice

Probate liquidity. That probably isn't something you think about every day. But certain lawyers do, and Rick Harmon of Probate Secrets Unlocked has learned how to offer his unique service in the "hard money" lending field (lending private funds) through local bar associations in Southern California.

"I kind of stumbled into a niche by speaking at a bar association," Rick recalls. "A couple of lawyers came up after a session and asked me if I could make a loan on a probate estate. I didn't know the answer at the time, but that question basically turned my business in that direction. Probate liquidity has been my niche for well over 20 years."

Rick markets his lending service through attorneys and other trusted advisors who refer their clients to him.

"My marketing has been aimed at influencing the attorneys by giving them the information they want and need," Rich explains. "I position myself as a peer, not as a vendor."

Rick gained this peer status with attorneys by joining local bar associations for attorneys who specialize in probate trust and estate planning. He also joined associations for paralegals and professional fiduciaries.

Attorneys are typically hungry for information, and Rick uses that to his advantage, offering to speak at meetings, writing articles for association publications, and publishing newsletters that he characterizes as "non-salesy."

"I really focus on trying to do the right thing rather than trying to sell lawyers or their clients something," Rick says. "That has built trust, which has become very profitable. I average $8,000.00 to $12,000.00 in profit per transaction, so when I get an attorney into my sales funnel as a referring source, the lifetime value of that referral source is extensive."

Endorsed Provider Marketing

"The swirl" is one of the things I talk about with Harley-Davidson dealers when I am coaching them to improve the profitability of their dealerships.

At any given time in a dealership, there are customers considering buying motorcycles, trying on clothes, or waiting for their motorcycles to be serviced; service techs working on motorcycles; parts orders arriving via UPS; and a parade of salespeople walking through the showroom. There are a hundred things the dealer would like to pay attention to, and at the end of the day, he's exhausted. He works hard every day, but he can't find time for the things that are most important because he is too busy.

That's the swirl. Perhaps you have it in your own business. So many different urgencies crop up that you aren't able to work on what's most important. It's like one of those shooting galleries at the fair. Targets pop up and you have to shoot them quickly before they disappear again. At the carnival you've got to concentrate on the gallery to score maximum points and get the biggest prize. It feels great when you hit all the targets, both at the carnival and in your business. When I get into the swirl in my own business, it actually feels good. It's like I'm the head of an army under attack. I've got projects and problems coming at me from all sides, and I've got to keep them all under control. While being in the swirl can feel invigorating, staying in the swirl is the wrong approach for a business owner.

Going back to my example about Harley-Davidson dealers, I taught them to create trackable goals for each department. Here is what I coached them to do:

Set your goals by first determining the total amount of money you want to make at the end of the year. Then assign a net profit contribution from each department. Based on that expectation, set goals for each month and what must be done within each department to achieve those goals. For instance, for motorcycle sales to generate the desired amount of profit, determine how many motorcycles the sales department needs to sell as a department. This will allow you to estimate the number of motorcycles each salesperson must sell each week to meet your goal.

Managing this way is like having a pause button for the swirl. You see that it exists, but it's happening to everyone else, not to you. That's because your attention isn't focused inside the swirl; instead, you can see all the way through it, straight to your goal. You are able to keep your attention on what's really important, driving your business toward your real business goals.

I'm sharing this to give you a pause button for the swirl. I've talked about a lot of different options, a lot of ways you can engage with associations, and I'm sure your head is swirling with possibilities. Let's slow down for a moment, now that you understand the basics, and take a long-range view. The goal you are trying to reach is an endorsed provider relationship.

An endorsed provider relationship gives the endorsed company access to an association's membership, along with the association's "seal of approval." Endorsed relationships are an excellent marketing method; however, I have seen too many companies work to create these relationships, expecting them to be the holy grail of niche marketing opportunities. Endorsed provider relationships are successful *only if built on top of an already successful association marketing program*.

From the association's perspective, I have seen association managers work for several years to find new endorsed provider opportunities where they can make a percentage of the revenue by providing the association's endorsement of the vendor. However, when these relationships are created solely for the benefit of generating a couple of dollars for the association or for a vendor trying to jump into an industry where he or she has never been before, they are rarely successful.

Before even considering an endorsed provider relationship, you should have already been to one or two annual meetings, sponsored an event, and perhaps exhibited at a trade show or participated in other programs and functions. Not only will all this activity have increased your visibility within the industry, it will also have given you the opportunity to develop a relationship with the staff of the association. That relationship is your key to initiating an endorsed provider relationship with an association. I've worked with several clients who created a successful endorsed provider relationship with an association who didn't yet have this level of experience. However, it's a lot easier if you've been participating in the association for some time. And if you aren't getting a good return on your investment from attending events and sponsorships, then you need to move on to another association that gives you a good ROI and is more suitable for creating an endorsed relationship.

As association managers consider your proposal for an endorsed provider relationship, they will be concerned that their rejection of your proposal will reduce your future participation in their events. Thus, they are going to take your offer more seriously than those offered by anyone else. So, not only will your endorsed provider relationship ultimately be more effective because you already have a relationship with the association and its staff, but you will also have a greater success rate in creating the endorsed provider relationship from the start.

In exchange for its endorsement, an association generally receives royalty payments. These royalties are for the use of the association's name, access to mailing lists, access to the association's staff, and endorsement letters for the vendor. In some cases, an association will send mailings on behalf of the vendor, provide free advertising in the association's publications, offer free booth space in trade shows, and even provide named sponsorship opportunities in exchange for those royalty payments.

Royalty payments are often calculated as a share of revenue generated through the endorsed provider relationship, so one of the benefits to the vendor is that becoming an endorsed provider is relatively inexpensive in the beginning because the starting volume is zero. The cost increases only as sales are generated.

While endorsed provider relationships will be detailed in a later chapter, it is important to note here that they are not the end goal. Sales are the end goal. Even if you obtain an association's endorsement and agreement to promote your products and services, the work is not over; it has just begun.

THE BIG PICTURE:
A FOUNDATION OF TERMS AND
INFORMATION TO
BUILD A NICHE MARKETING PLAN

Associations are as diverse as the markets they serve. Associations and their staffs range in size from large organizations with hundreds of employees, to those with 5 to 10 employees, to a great many with just one employee, to many others that are volunteer-run and have no employees working on a day-to-day basis at the association's headquarters. While many associations represent businesses and industries, many others represent individuals, and while one association may have only a few members in a state, others represent millions located around the world.

Trade and Professional Associations
There are primarily two different types of associations that represent two different groups of businesses and individuals. Associations that represent retailers, contractors, manufacturers, distributors, and other

types of businesses are called trade associations. Trade associations are not-for-profit organizations that are groups of competitors that have come together to improve their industry. Trade associations are nonprofit extensions of the for-profit world, often providing these industries with critical business information, opportunities for education, and political representation that is too costly for any one company to provide on an individual basis. In addition, these organizations are much more effective at accomplishing goals on behalf of an industry than any one member of the industry could be on its own.

Trade associations usually provide their members with education programming, meetings, trade shows, and other industry-specific events for members to improve their skills and improve their services to their customers. They will often have industry-specific newsletters, publications, and email broadcasts, and they will serve as a forum for members to share experiences and problems with others in their industry. Most trade associations represent 1,000 to 2,000 companies, but certainly there are those that represent several thousand, including some that represent more than 100,000 companies within an industry. Then there are those that represent only one or two dozen companies within a field.

The second type of association is known as a professional association or an individual membership society. These organizations represent individuals or professionals within a field. Members usually share common professions, like interests, and similar objectives, and they are often composed of individuals who have specific knowledge or expertise that qualifies them to be part of the profession. Membership in the association is often limited to those who have obtained specific professional credentials that allow them to practice within a particular field.

These organizations carry on many of the same functions as trade groups, except they are formed on behalf of individuals instead of companies. Professional associations or individual societies range from huge organizations, such as AARP (formerly known as the American Association of Retired Persons), to societies that represent specific vocations or professions on a national, regional, or even municipal basis.

National, State, and Local Associations

While many of the associations you commonly think of are household names and represent members throughout the world, or certainly throughout the country, the majority of the associations in the United States represent a specific state or a local area.

While these organizations are often independent, other times they are related through a chapter system with other associations. The relationships between national, state, and local chapters and affiliates are important to understand, for they often influence the consideration and development of any product or service you plan to market.

Many times you will find you can start with a national association to develop a relationship, and it will filter down to the state and regional societies. Other times you will find a national association can actually provide you as a resource to its state or regional chapters. Sometimes you will find the chapters are simply uncooperative and not interested in what the national organization has to say. In those cases, it may be best to work through each of the city, regional, and state societies and work your way up to the national office. Most important, you need to keep in mind that these groups are often distinct organizations with their own politics and decision-making authority.

Association Sections and Councils

It may be hard to believe, but many associations find it important to subdivide their industry by individuals or groups of companies that have a similar interest or need within their memberships. Unless they are diverse and arcane associations, how could you possibly need further divisions within an industry? With that said, many new splinter organizations have been created that further subdivide an association's membership into smaller groups of individuals with more specialized interests and needs.

In an effort to increase their relevance, associations have created special sections or councils within their own memberships. These sections can be formed around special disciplines within an industry, they can be arranged around the business size of members, or they can be arranged around particular disciplines or subspecialties within a profession.

Councils and sections allow members who share common interests and specialties to exchange ideas and techniques specific to their area of expertise. Many of these sections and councils provide unique educational opportunities and government representation for their subspecialty. In addition, these sections and councils provide a trained group of individuals ready to help the parent organization with identified future leaders within a profession.

When they were first formed, associations typically charged an extra fee to participate in these councils and sections; however, the trend has turned, and most associations now include section participation in their regular membership dues. These sections and councils can provide an even better niche marketing opportunity because their interests are more clearly defined. The groups are smaller, and it will be easier for you to identify yourself with each group and its goals more quickly. You should examine the list of problems you created (see page 17) to see if any of the special interest groups would be particularly interested in the problems you are able to solve.

Special Interest Associations

Even though many associations are creating special interest sections within their memberships, they have not been able to stop the trend of separate special interest associations forming. Very often these associations are formed when a special interest group is not happy with the level of representation or support it is getting from the national organization. Often these groups are on the cusp of new technological advancements or new marketing enhancements within an industry. Many times the "old guard" of the large national association will be threatened by these new developments and will stifle their development within the larger association. These specialized organizations can be a lucrative opportunity for the association marketer. Since they are often much newer in their development cycle than their larger counterparts, these specialty organizations are much more appreciative of the support they get from vendors to the industry.

Practical Examples

Let's say you can solve a problem for physicians throughout the country and have decided you want to create a niche-marketing program for physicians. You can target these physicians through a variety of associations.

First, there is the national American Medical Association (AMA). This organization represents physicians nationwide. It has its own meetings, newsletters, and education programs for members that are interested in national issues affecting the broad profession of medicine.

In addition to the AMA, state medical societies represent every state in the country. Therefore, you will find groups of individuals, many of them AMA members, who also participate in state societies. These societies have their own sets of newsletters, education, and programming for physicians within their states. And that is not to mention the city organizations that also represent physicians. Not all cities have medical societies, but many do.

In addition to the national, state, and city societies for general medicine, there are national specialty societies such as the American Academy of Dermatology, the American College of Obstetrics and Gynecology, and the American Society of Anesthesiologists, to name just three. Now, you will find that many of the members of those societies are, in fact, members of the American Medical Association, but many times they are not. While some physicians are interested in knowing about general medical issues, others choose to have their information filtered by their specialty society so it is specifically applicable to their particular needs. In addition to national specialty societies, specialists are represented on a state level by state societies in most of the states. For instance, there is a Florida Society of Dermatology. In addition to those state specialty societies, there are subspecialty societies within those organizations as well. There is a Florida Society of Dermatological Surgery, for instance.

Each of these organizations has its own media, its own events, and its own education programming. As a marketer, you need to be aware that each of these organizations exists, each provides unique opportunities for you to market your goods and services, and each can be replaced. If you find that one organization is not cooperative, move on, because many others within that same industry may be perfectly open to your participation.

As you examine the association market, your success will depend not only on how targeted your marketing becomes, but also on how you select the associations you will target. Your understanding of the structure of the association industry is just the first step toward understanding how they make decisions and how they can be influenced to work with you.

Speaking for Associations Is a
Shortcut to Success

Tracey Fieber is a business consultant who generates clients for her company, Tracey Fieber Business Solutions, by speaking at association events. Her process is simple and direct. And it works.

"Everything we do is focused on business growth," Tracey says. "We help some companies in the area of hiring and team building. For others, it's in the area of marketing online and/or offline. And then for others it's about operational processes and automating. Typically we end up helping a business in all three areas."

Tracey finds companies that need her expertise through associations. She and her team developed their list of associations to target the old fashioned way—they went to the library and did research. Armed with their list, they mailed letters and followed up with telephone calls, offering Tracey as a speaker for association events.

Those speaking engagements help to position Tracey as an expert, and she includes a call to action with each one.

"The type of group determines what our call to action is," Tracey explains. "Sometimes we have people sign up for our newsletter so we can develop relationships and then move forward. Other times, we make the offer to sign up for consultation right there."

Tracey says using associations is the fastest way to get in front of groups of people.

"It can be very lucrative," she says, "and it's a great way to grow your business."

THE INSIDE SECRETS OF
ASSOCIATION MANAGEMENT

When my daughter, Samantha, was 13 years old, she came home angry one day. She was so frustrated with her friends that she stopped playing four-square. It's a game they play at school with four players who try to get each other out by bouncing the ball into an opponent's square in a way that she cannot return it to another player's square. Kind of like a four-player tennis match with a big rubber ball. Samantha wanted her mother and me to intervene at school on her behalf. It may not seem like much, but evidently, four-square is an important sport. (Her school has banned dodge ball, but I'll save that for another forum.)

My daughter believes that players should get two bounces of the ball before returning it to another player. If you aren't up on your four-square rules, the rules specify one bounce and then you have to return the ball; two bounces and you're out. To mix things up one afternoon, they played with two bounces to return; three bounces and you're out. Now Samantha thinks this is the way four-square should be played.

A dispute erupted at school. Samantha tried to convince her friends to play four-square with two bounces. They weren't having any of it. The coach got involved and explained that four-square is a one-bounce game. Samantha stormed off. She didn't want to play. Her friends played four-square in the customary fashion. Most appeared to enjoy it. My daughter sat alone and brooded because she believes that's not the way four-square should be played. And then she came home angry about it.

"That's not the way four-square should be," she told me through tears of frustration. "With two bounces it's fairer to all the kids who can't get to the ball on one bounce. This way no one person dominates the game, and more people get a turn."

My typical fatherly response was, "Get out there and play; the rules are the rules. If that's the way the game is played, get out there and play the game without worrying about the way it should be. Just play the game the way it is."

"But that's not fair." she protested. "Two bounces is better. It's easier for everyone, and it's a lot more fun. I'd rather sit out than play in a game that's so unfair."

When life isn't going your way, the immediate reaction is to wish it were different. Maybe even try to demand that it *be* different. Reality can be harsh, and it can be frustrating to realize a situation isn't the way you expected it to be. Before you know it, you're grumbling about how it *should* be done.

Seeing things as they are allows you to adapt, creating a positive environment for success. Wishing things were different is a trap that prevents you from devising solutions.

The companies I work with to create association marketing plans have expectations for what associations should do or could do to promote their products and services. Often these expectations are unrealistic.

They exclaim, "That's stupid! It would be so much easier if the association would just …"

Perhaps, but that's not the way it works in the association world. You've got to play by their rules—or go home angry.

It's critical to understand how associations operate. Since I am an association industry insider, allow me to give you a peek inside, to give you a better understanding of the needs, expectations, and capabilities of the associations with which you'll be working.

Learning the standard decision-making process that associations go through to choose education programs, to select vendors, or to authorize endorsed provider relationships requires an understanding of the decision-making buyers within the association itself.

Membership

The membership has the ultimate decision-making authority within an association. A decision by the membership requires compliance from all members of the board of directors and staff. However, very few decisions are brought to the entire membership for consideration.

Typically the entire membership of an association meets only annually. At its annual meeting, the membership considers any bylaws changes that have been proposed, any broad-range decisions that are affecting the industry as a whole, and the election of the officers and the board of directors. Beyond that, the membership as a whole does not generally meet and make decisions.

Board of Directors

Almost all the large decisions within an association are made by its board of directors. The association's board will meet anywhere from once a year, to twice a year, to quarterly, to even monthly. These boards may wrestle with issues ranging from the main legislative proposals affecting the industry to color choices on the walls at the association's headquarters. As you consider working with an association, if you can become a member, you will be granted access to the membership's meetings, or you can request minutes of the board of directors' meetings. This will offer an unparalleled resource for you to gain understanding of exactly which types of decisions the board of directors is making. Also as an associate member, even if you are not invited to serve on the board of directors, you often will be permitted to attend the board's meetings. This is a great way to see for yourself the type of information being presented to the board so you can judge if this is the body that needs to approve your proposals or if you should be focusing primarily on the association's staff. By being in the room, you'll learn interesting information, and you'll be able to meet several potential, influential customers.

Staff

Although an association's staff members will often put you off by saying they need to take a proposal to their board of directors or they need an officer's approval, quite honestly the top staff members typically can achieve whatever they want to accomplish within the association. More often than not, the main decision-makers within an industry are the staff members at the association's headquarters. There was an extensive debate 5 to 10 years ago about whether associations should be staff-driven or member-driven organizations. The fact is associations already are staff driven and probably always will be staff driven. This is critical for you to understand as an association marketer. While we will discuss plenty of techniques you can use if the association's staff is not cooperative with your goals, it is more productive to work with associations whose staff members are willing and eager to work with you.

The Top Three Daily Frustrations of Association Staff

1. The Board of Directors

No one has such a unique perspective as does the association executive. Association executives get to hear the insights, if they are listening, of some of the best and the brightest performers within their industry. They see the perspective of vendors who are selling to the industry. And they also hear directly from the regulators who are overseeing the industry. While individuals within the industry who have volunteered to serve on the board of directors always do it with the best intentions, they may not have the best perspective for making decisions on behalf of the organization. Or they may not even have the perspective necessary for making the best decisions on behalf of the industry. Thus, association executives are eternally frustrated with the decisions made by the board of directors. Boards are often subject to group thinking mentality, where the last thing said just before the vote is the thing that sways the vote. A board of directors very rarely makes a divisive or a split decision. More often than not, the members will work to find a compromise solution that everyone can support. All this does is water down solutions and keep the board from addressing the most significant problems within an industry. Hard decisions are generally left for another day.

This creates a lot of frustration for association executives because, to them, these decisions are easy. They clearly see what the industry must do, and they do not understand why the board of directors does not readily share that view. The board members, of course, discount the association executive's opinion, because the executive does not actually own a company within that industry. They say, "Yeah, it's easy for him (or her) to want that. He does not have to live by that new law or that way of doing business or that certification program. It's easy for him to suggest it."

A lot of wasted energy is spent on managing this friction between the board members' perception of their industry as operators within it and the association executive's perspective as someone outside of the day-to-day business, but who is an insider from the standpoint of having comprehensive, albeit secondhand, information gleaned from the industry's participants.

2. Profound Fear

Association executives are deathly afraid of being embarrassed. The range of expertise they must possess to be effective association managers is more diverse than any other profession I have experienced. They must be experts in meeting management, government affairs, public relations, employment matters, board relations, and negotiations, and have a nice, charming personality. And this does not include the industry- or profession-specific information on which they are expected to be experts. If they are working with the Pool and Spa Association, for instance, they need to know every regulation and every law that has anything to do with pool contractors and be able to recite them off the top of their head, they must know the critical vendors, they must understand the large companies, and they must also know the leaders within the smaller companies. All this must be acquired and perfected within the first 90 days of employment.

Because of the breadth of knowledge required, association executives realize they know very little in-depth about any one of those areas. Thus, they live in fear of mishandling employment law issues or organizational issues such as bylaws and articles of incorporation. Much of their work is involved in learning their particular industry, focusing on effective negotiations for education venues, and working with speakers to create inspired education programs. They cannot spend the time necessary to become experts in many of the other areas of their expected knowledge domain. So they are constantly worried that they may have forgotten something or that something being presented to them could be dangerous to them or to their organization. The most embarrassing thing that can happen to association executives is to be caught off guard by some form they were supposed to file or some project they were supposed to complete, things they should have done because anybody with the least amount of knowledge in employment law would have known you have to do. Now they must sit in front of their board and explain why they need to find room in the budget for a huge penalty the association must pay for missing a deadline.

So, any new proposal, any new event, any new opportunity for the association must be filtered through this fear the association executive has about the unknown and the potential issues that could arise from that unknown. You will often hear from association executives, "Oh, we can't do that because we are tax exempt. It's against our nonprofit status." Well, we are going to talk about those things in this manual. Sometimes an association executive's concerns are grounded in fact, but more often they are grounded in plain, old-fashioned fear.

3. Overwhelming Demands
The volume of people contacting an association manager is staggering. Now, remember, these individuals are basically "just employees," but they are employees who have responsibility for an entire industry or profession. Not only do they have all the members and potential members calling them, they have business vendors, hotels trying to get them to bring their education events to their venues, affiliate organizations, and government regulators all calling them and asking for information or help. It is well engrained into every association executive's mind that under no circumstances are they ever to say no to anyone.

These executives are forever trying to fulfill every request presented to them, to create every report any committee asks of them, and to be polite to anyone who calls. It is an overwhelming amount of work to take on, and the range of expertise necessary to accomplish those goals is as diverse as any I have seen within any industry. So, the first thing to understand about association executives is that they are unbelievably overwhelmed and in over their head. It is critical to keep this in mind as you contact an association manager with an idea or a proposal.

KEY MOTIVATIONS OF ASSOCIATION EXECUTIVES

Allow me to open up associations, pop the hood so to speak and show you what is underneath, to give you some insight into what association leaders are thinking about on a daily basis.

Member Value – Return on Investment for Membership Dues

The primary consideration through which associations filter all their programs and activities is the members' perceived return on investment for paying their membership dues. Thus, every new program, every new meeting, every government affairs initiative is created because the association's leadership is striving to justify the membership dues. It used to be that association executives could count on a large base of members to participate in the association because that is what you are supposed to do within an industry. Today, however, more and more associations are being held up to a "value microscope," where members are closely analyzing the return on investment they receive from paying dues to the organization. For many association members, it is no longer "a given" to pay dues just because the association does good things on behalf of the industry or the profession. Many individuals require direct benefits to accrue to them by virtue of their participation as members, or they don't join. Association executives call these individuals "free riders." They do not participate in the association, but they benefit from the association's government affairs activities and other industrywide initiatives.

Increasingly, association executives are getting caught in the trap of trying to attract non-members to join the association by listening to their current members and doing more of the activities their current members suggest they do. This might be a great membership retention strategy for the members they already have, but many times it only serves to alienate the association further from its potential members.

While it is important for you to understand that association executives are constantly striving to generate stronger membership numbers, it is equally important to recognize that certain individuals within an industry will almost always choose to participate in the association, but others will not.

Another area that generates a lot of attention from association executives is government relations. This is the primary function for many associations. While they have education programs and perhaps even newsletters, the primary reason for their existence is to conduct government relations activities on behalf of their members. You will be able to identify these organizations by reviewing their board meeting minutes from the last several meetings. If their meetings devote a large amount of time to different regulatory agencies' and legislators' initiatives that they are debating, discussing, drafting, redrafting, revising, building consensus on, and then proposing and counter-proposing, you will get a quick sense that this is one of those organizations.

The more you understand about the association's government relations activities, the more you are going to be able to talk knowledgeably with members. The association will appreciate someone from outside the industry who helps the organization with its government affairs goals. Whether it is participating in meetings, sharing expertise, or providing funding for the government relations programs, you can make a lot of great friends in an industry by helping them with the lawmaking process.

Technology is playing a huge role in today's associations. The leaders are not only concerned with the efficient use of technology by their organizations, but they are also focused on the technological developments within their industries and professions. More and more associations are looking for technological solutions that can help them provide their content in a variety of ways. They are conducting online training, providing web seminars for their members, as well as conducting conference calls for educational purposes and to communicate with leaders. If you have an idea for providing content for the association that helps with the government relations goal or provides more member value, and also uses a technological advancement the association has not already incorporated, your proposal will likely meet with success.

Associations spend a good deal of time on concerns associated with the scrutiny and the compliance of their own organization. They are very sensitive to criticism from both members and outsiders, such as government regulators or lawmakers, and especially the press. This makes associations very risk-adverse and prone to passing on an otherwise good opportunity if there is concern that someone will be frustrated or upset with the association if it acts on the proposal. Since many associations are tax-exempt entities, they are subject to the scrutiny of the Internal Revenue Service. In addition, the Federal Trade Commission responds to complaints from association members or potential members about possible antitrust violations that could be occurring within an association. And the press, both the popular press and the industry-specific press, is forever scrutinizing the activities in which these organizations engage.

Add to that the fact that board members, while they may be experts in their particular industry, are not altogether familiar with the unique scrutiny that associations face. This makes them even more risk-adverse because of the concern that an action could bring negative consequences to the association.

It used to be that associations operated without any competition for members. Individuals within an industry felt some level of obligation to join their industry association. They participated in their organization by attending the events and the education, and they gave very little thought to the value they derived from it. Today, associations must compete in the marketplace to build and maintain their memberships.

Not only are associations competing against other organizations offering association programs, either on a regional, state, or national level, but they must also compete with for-profit providers offering "problem-solving" solutions to the association's potential members. Thus, associations increasingly have to study and respond to competitive pressure, both from other associations as well as from for-profit service providers offering benefits to their potential members.

Associations are always looking for new revenue sources. While membership dues is still the largest segment of an association's spendable dollars, associations are usually open to non-dues revenue opportunities. If an organization is able to offer more membership benefits and generate new revenue for the organization, this is a double win opportunity about which they will be very excited.

Associations make a huge investment to provide education programs and in-person meetings for their members. Larger associations may have several full-time employees dedicated to producing one annual meeting, usually a three- or a four-day event. It is daunting when you consider the logistics, communication, and coordination necessary to put on one of these events. It really is a wonder that so many of them take place each year.

While it might seem simple to suggest an add-on event for one evening or another half-hour session one day during the meeting, many different considerations and coordination must go into executing that decision. It might be a great idea and the leadership might be for it, but it can create a lot of frustration on the part of the in-line employees who must implement it.

If small organizations tracked the hours employees spend on each of the tasks in their program areas, they would find they spend one-third to one-half of their time putting on in-person education programs for their members. The financial success of these events is critical to the long-term welfare of the association, and association leaders are always eager to find new ideas and new programs that will attract registrants, exhibitors, and sponsors to their events.

Associations share a challenge with private industry in that they are constantly concerned about workforce issues. There is a limited number of individuals who even know what an association is, much less understand how to plan a meeting or run a government affairs program. And those individuals are hard to find. Then, once an association has hired an employee, it has the same motivation and supervision issues found in any employer-employee relationship.

Add to that the challenge of a board of directors that gets together only periodically, but has to monitor, evaluate, and supervise the performance of the executive director, and it creates a huge burden and amount of stress on the part of everyone involved.

Associations frequently form alliances with other industries and organizations. A significant amount of time is invested into generating positive relationships with other stakeholders within an industry. Every industry association has vendors and groups of customers to which it needs to respond, and the other associations representing each of those customers and vendors are good allies for the industry association. A lot of time is invested into creating and nurturing these coalitions and alliances for the benefit of all industry participants.

In the end, associations work hard to create a favorable impression on everyone. They want their members to feel good about the association so they will pay membership dues. They also want their members to attend the association's events, be happy they attended, and want to come to future events the association may hold. They want vendors to feel good about the trade show and want to come back, and they want sponsors not only to support this year's event, but also to sponsor every future event they may decide to create. Associations face tremendous pressure to please and to create a good impression with every member, every potential ally, every government official, every hotel salesperson, and every "anyone else" who may call the office or have an interaction with the association. As a rule, associations are concerned with making sure that everyone who sends the association money, or could send the association money in the future, or could be valuable to its members has a favorable, memorable experience with the organization.

No Matter How You Say It, Association Meetings Are Where the Customers Are

The recent financial downturn hit the automobile industry especially hard, and Beverly Wall's Languages International, a foreign language agency in Detroit, was hit right along with it. So, she turned to associations to generate new customers.

Beverly's main customers are manufacturers that ship products to countries where people do not speak English.

"We do business in 80 different languages," she explains. "We translate, we interpret, we teach, we do graphic design; we do all the things that touch foreign language."

Beverly has developed relationships with the organizations that assist manufacturers in exporting their products.

"The key is to be in the room," she says, "so I sponsor seminars, breakfasts, and other events. Exporting is like a domino game. Eventually the manufacturer will need to translate information to other languages. I just have to wait for people to get to the translation part, and then it's like, 'Hi, I'm here to help you!' That's what has helped my company the most, being associated with the group that helps people export."

Beverly says associations will "take anybody's money" to sponsor events, and she has found herself marketing in a competitor-free zone.

"I don't know why my competition is not there," she says, "but that's O.K. I just make my materials available, and people come up to me and say, 'Oh you're the translation part. I'm going to need you at some point.' It creates a nice connection so when they get to the translation part of the process, I don't have any competition."

Making Yourself Into Someone Associations Eagerly WANT to Work With

I first noticed it in my dad's tire store. I worked there during summer vacations from high school, changing tires and doing oil changes. There were some guys in the shop who worked hard and got a lot done, and then there were others who smoked cigarettes more than they worked on cars.

Because the hard workers were almost always prompt in the morning and worked hard throughout the day, my dad gave them the most slack on the days they were late or the times they wanted to take their kids to the doctor's office. The guys who didn't work as hard got sent home or were in trouble if they were just a couple minutes late one morning.

I took this lesson to heart and applied it to all my work. In my first professional job, I quickly decided I'd do the work of three or four people. I didn't mind. I figured the more jobs I did, the harder it would be to replace me. By doing those jobs, I learned a lot I never would have known otherwise, and soon I was efficient enough to get it all done.

I often hear from companies looking to build a relationship with an association, "It's taking forever; how do I get them to make a decision?"

The key element in any relationship is trust. Can the association trust you to take care of its members, perform as you've promised, and provide the benefit the association is promoting to its members? You must build that trust, and then the association will want to make a decision quickly for fear it will lose you as a valued partner.

Associations want free content that will justify membership dues and generate additional revenue for the association. There are many ways you can help an association approach that ideal scenario while opening the door to profitable marketing opportunities for yourself. Let me describe a handful.

You should join as an associate or affiliate member any organization you are targeting. Not only will this give you credibility and recognition within that organization, but it will also give you valuable information about your targeted industry or profession, even if the organization's projects and services are not up to par with other organizations and you feel like you are wasting your dues investment. A poorly run organization can provide you as important a lesson in marketing as a well run organization can provide. Joining an association puts you on the mailing list for the organization's newsletters and meeting announcements. You should read each of them in detail because they contain hints that explain to you exactly what is going on in the industry, who the main players are, who the influencers are, and who you need to meet and work with in that group or niche.

If you are reading a meeting brochure and any of the speakers are prospects for your products or services, you need to target those individuals directly. If they are adequately impressed with what you have to offer, they may mention you during their program. Those speakers, whether they are outside experts or industry insiders, are the influencers of decisions, at least during that meeting. The association's members are going to be taking those speakers to dinner, taking them to lunch, or speaking with them after the meeting, and you want those decision influencers to be aware of you, your products, and your services. Membership in the organization is the only thing that will ensure you have the basic foundation of information you need to reach a particular niche of individuals.

Meeting attendance is also an important step to reaching a target market. Association meetings pull together many individuals from within an industry. Yes, plenty of people choose not to attend the association's meetings, and yes, they are important customers you could be reaching in other ways, but you should not ignore the low-hanging fruit—the members who attend the association's events. You should work with those individuals first, make sure you gain an understanding of the industry or the profession, and then use that understanding during one-on-one sales calls with individuals who choose not to attend the association's meeting. You will always be more effective after going to meetings and gaining more understanding of your target market.

Here are two important things you need to do when you attend an association's events:

1. **Attend a significant amount of the education.** I am not suggesting you have to go to every breakout session—most of the content will not be exceptionally relevant to you as a vendor—but do attend a good portion of the programming, sit near the front, find out who is asking questions, find out who is offering additional information, and learn everything you can about the audience you are seeking. By the end of the program, you may know as much about the issues and changes affecting the industry as the industry's participants do.

2. **Hang out in the hallways.** Look for small groups of people who have gathered outside the meeting room and try to introduce yourself to them. Many times they are outside the meeting room because they believe they have heard it all already—and perhaps they have. Maybe they are the old-timers who have been to lots of meetings, and they gain more value from interacting with other participants than they do from attending the education program. They are important people to approach to make sure they have an understanding of your products and services.

Quite frankly, there is just no more efficient means of contacting and networking with association members than attending their events. You can do in-person sales calls or telephone marketing for a long time and not build the relationships you can in a two-day meeting or even a one-day meeting within a niche industry.

To Exhibit or Not to Exhibit

I do not want to dissuade you from exhibiting if you believe it can benefit you. Many products and services sell very well through an exhibit booth. However, before you invest the money for an exhibit, if you are at all leery about the value of that investment, or about your abilities or investment to create a booth, you ought to attend the event as a regular registrant first. Exhibiting puts you on the same aisle with your competitors and other individuals, all trying to reach the same market. This can be both effective and ineffective at the same time.

If you are a smaller player, exhibiting puts you in the marketplace. Yes, it is a good opportunity for you to be seen, and there you are. It is the only forum where you can have a multimillion-dollar booth with all sorts of lights and signs and beautiful carpeting, amenities, and fixtures next to or down the aisle from a mom and pop operation that has a table with two chairs and a pile of brochures. It allows you to boost yourself to the middle of the industry by writing one check.

However, spending an entire meeting sitting behind a table or standing in a booth, or even if you are out in the aisle of a trade show, is not necessarily the most productive use of your time. If the bulk of the attendees are in an education session, then you should be there, too.

Yes, you will have to listen to the speaker for 45 minutes or an hour, and during that time you won't be talking to anyone, but the five minutes you spend talking to the person on your left and right immediately before the program, and perhaps exchanging cards with them at the end of the program, is two prospects an hour you wouldn't have generated on the exhibit floor. Plus, the investment is much lower.

Associations like to promote special deals for their members. This helps to justify the association's existence and the members' membership dues. If you can create a special offer or a discount or additional bonuses that go along with a product or a service created especially for the members, you will find the association very willing to help you promote them. While many associations will simply ask you to go ahead and buy advertising, others will be happy to promote your offers in a listing of membership benefits or other media they are sending to potential or current members. The more you can tailor your offer to the specific audience at a meeting or within an association's membership, the better results you will have. Remember, people are always filtering the messages they hear, both consciously and subconsciously. The first step to getting a new customer is to get him or her to pay attention to you. Only then do you have the opportunity to tell your sales story. The special offer you create for an association's membership does two things. One, it gives the association something it can promote, and two, it customizes your message to the target audience.

Associations are constantly searching for new content for their education programs. It can be content gleaned from other meetings, content that is broken out into new specialty seminars, or content delivered via teleconference calls or even special publications. Generally the programs for large meetings are developed by a committee of volunteers within the association. The association executive typically guards this committee from any outside interference or marketing opportunities, with one exception. If you are a member of the association, usually you will be invited to participate in the education committee meetings. The education committee discusses all the potential ideas for an education program, prioritizes them, and selects presenters. If you cannot participate in these planning sessions, then your avenue for getting on the program is right back with the staff person handling the event. Very often, that staff person will tell you he or she took your information to the committee, the committee prioritized all the potential options, and unfortunately it decided not to include your presentation. Let me tell you, if the staff person wanted you on the program, you would be on the program, so the quickest way to be included is through that staff person.

Now that staff person probably has several other people clamoring to get on the program as well. Association executives will always give preference to customized content that has not been heard at any other event. Speakers commonly have lists of prepared presentations that come as a package and even post them on their websites—like a McDonald's menu board. Generally speaking, most people are turned off by what appears to be "canned" content when they are choosing what to include in their program. While it is good for a speaker to package his or her content, association executives are always looking for fresh, never-delivered-before material.

I am not saying you must create new content for every event you do, but you need to be aware that organizations are looking for fresh content, so you should position whatever you are presenting as the newest, latest, and greatest information necessary for their members' success.

When the staff's meeting planner is developing the program for an event in cooperation with the education committee, there is a hierarchy of speakers the staff prefers. Number one, meeting planners prefer speakers who are able to deliver excellent content for little or no cost. And if those content providers are also going to sponsor a function or exhibit in the trade show, that is all the better for the meeting planner.

The next level of speaker preference includes the ones for which the association has to pay travel expenses, but do not demand an honorarium to come. Lawmakers and government bureaucrats often fit into this category.

The third level of preference is for speakers that demand both an honorarium and travel expenses to come to an event. While most meeting planners do have a budget for speakers' fees and expenses, generally they are terribly averse to actually spending money to bring in speakers. There are so many internal industry content providers that associations rarely have to pay someone to come.

After the program is 95 percent developed, there very well may be holes or small opportunities to drop in speakers, and this is actually a very good way to position yourself as a vendor trying to market him or herself to an industry. If you take the pressure off, and simply say, "Hey, if you have a hole you are trying to fill and are looking for terrific content to provide your membership that will be a great drawing card and attract more attendees to your meeting, I have a program you will probably be interested in," this information will be very good news to most association executives.

Now, what if the meeting has been filled and you were left out? Well, one of the underused methods of getting in front of an association's membership and being recognized as an industry expert is creating a standalone event away from the meetings the association usually provides. I had seen it before, but Dan Kennedy was the first person I heard teach this method.

Very often, you will be able to work with an association that will accept you as a content provider and create an entire one-day or two-day seminar around you. You will need to develop the content and probably write most of the marketing copy for a brochure to explain the benefits attendees will experience by attending your event. But since you are speaking at the association's event, the association will take the lead on marketing. It will be the association's responsibility to distribute brochures throughout the industry, take registrations, and handle all the on-site logistics for the program. For this, you deliver the program, and the association gets to keep the revenue, often with a revenue split with you.

As a presenter, you get the credibility of being held out by the association as an expert about your topic, you get to meet all the participants who register for the event, and you walk away with the leftover brochures to show other prospects that you are an industry expert. These brochures are an effective way to approach other associations when you are pitching yourself as a speaker for their events or as a speaker for a standalone event they should organize for their members.

Becoming a content provider that offers a message specific to an organization's membership is perhaps the most efficient way to use associations to gain credibility, awareness of your products and services, and market share within a particular niche.

Associations are always looking for additional content for their publications. Many of them have websites and newsletters they use to communicate information to their members. Very often, the editor of the newsletter is searching for content that is specific enough for the industry and yet easy and inexpensive to obtain. Any time you are writing a newsletter article, you need to write it from the perspective of solving a problem that exists within the industry. If you follow this formula, you will get a large number of your articles published in associations' newsletters:

1. Document a problem that is widespread within an industry, and provide a couple of case examples of how that problem hurts members within the industry.
2. Compare and contrast a number of possible solutions to that problem, giving the benefits and challenges of each of those solutions.

3. Provide a couple of case scenarios of organizations within the industry that had the problem and then solved it using one of the various methods.
4. Provide a conclusion as to which solution seems to work best for the industry.

After you have drafted the article, submit it to the association with a tag line at the bottom that provides some information about you and your company, as well as your contact information in case someone is interested in reaching you for additional information.

Do not be overwhelmed by this process. It is a terrific opportunity!

If you are not sure what sort of problems you should write about, break out your association membership directory, or the board of directors listing if you do not have a list of all the members, and call as many as you can. Tell them you are writing an article for the association's newsletter, and you want to ask them what their top three daily frustrations are in their business life.

This tactic will not only give you valuable ideas for your newsletter article, it will also give you the opportunity to speak in a non-threatening and even helpful way with the leaders of the industry. This will give you increased credibility with these association members.

Now take the ideas you have garnered, devise ways you and your product can solve some of those problems, and do another round of telephone interviews to discuss ways people have either dealt with the problems or solved those problems. While making all those calls might seem unproductive, they will give you a tremendous amount of information about your customers and give you notoriety within the industry at the same time.

As your experience with an industry grows and you become better known, it may be a good idea to begin exhibiting at the industry association's events. This will be an opportunity to show you are among the industry's supporters. The association's leaders will see you want to be a part of the organization and that you support their efforts on behalf of members.

If you choose to exhibit, one of the most important things you can do is marketing follow-up, both before and after the show. Follow-up is what separates the successful vendors from the unsuccessful ones. Sure, there is a lot for you to do during the event to make sure your display is as nice as it should be and you are communicating an effective message to your target audience. But the most important thing to do is follow-up: to make sure people know you are going to be at the show, to get them to make it a point to come and see you at the event, to follow up with any sales or commitments you make, and to turn any prospects you meet into customers.

Another opportunity to gain goodwill and support within an industry is to sponsor an event or a function. Sponsors are often introduced and recognized for their support during the course of an event, and these opportunities provide you with positive exposure among the industry's participants. Sponsorship recognition can vary as much as the organizations that offer these opportunities. When you are a meeting attendee, before you have decided to sponsor, watch how the organization recognizes its sponsors. Since you will have seen the sponsorship fees in the meeting's promotional materials, you will be able to judge the cost of the recognition versus the benefit you will accrue from participating. It can be a very valuable position to be a sponsor at an event, but you ought to know in advance the recognition and benefits you will receive from your investment.

You can also create your own event within an association's program. If an association has chosen not to have a dinner, it may be a good idea for you to host a dinner, if not for everyone attending the meeting, then for a select few people you want to invite. Many times you will find the association is willing to promote an event that you hold outside of the normal program. However, if the association is going to promote your event, it will probably have to be open to all members.

One of the ways that new vendors interact with associations is by helping the organization develop fresh and entirely new content it can deliver to its membership. This content can be in the form of books, manuals, DVDs, or teleconference calls the association can deliver to its members as a membership benefit. Providing content is a tremendous opportunity for you to promote awareness and build the credibility of your name, products, and services, because the association is distributing, and thus tacitly endorsing, your content to its members. The members view your information as valuable content they have paid for with their membership dues. As the members become engaged with your content, their perceived value of you as an expert grows.

One of the innovative ways I have seen consultants work with associations is to become an "expert-on-call" for an association's members. Typically the vendor-consultant charges a fee to the association, usually a nominal amount, that allows the association's members to contact the vendor directly if they have questions. The consultant offers an introductory level of service, perhaps a telephone consultation that allows members to call in, ask questions, and get meaningful answers for their everyday concerns. An example of this is Seay Management Consultants, a firm that operates a labor information line for associations. Associations can pay a small fee, usually around $150.00 a month, for the consultant-on-call service. The association publicizes the consultant-on-call service to its members as a membership benefit. When members call, they are provided with an excellent array of employment-related consultant services, and whenever the need arises, Seay Management stands ready to help the member with a wage and hour audit, an OSHA inspection, or a defense against a sexual harassment complaint on a fee-for-service basis. These arrangements provide a win/win/win: Associations have a benefit they can market to their members; the members receive free telephone consulting for everyday needs and a proven resource for more extensive needs; and the consultant benefits from a moderate stream of revenue as well as having the association serve the role of promoting the company's services to a niche market.

Another way you can help an association and yourself is by hosting your own meetings. When you as an associate member express interest in hosting a regional or a local meeting, most associations will be receptive to that opportunity. You will need to secure a location, determine a date and time, and find a speaker (usually other than yourself), and then go to the association to pitch the meeting as an opportunity to offer an additional membership benefit. Here is the pitch:

> I have a great speaker lined up who will cover [content generally needed by the members]. I will cover the expenses because I understand how important this is to the industry. Would you be interested in promoting it to your membership? (If they say yes, great. You continue with your pitch.) Could you see your way clear to list me as a sponsor? I will take care of your RSVPs, and if you promote the event within your newsletter and perhaps send a special mailing to members in the area, I will pick up the cost of the speaker and the event.

This is an offer few associations are able to refuse, and if you find a couple that do refuse it, keep going until you find someone interested and willing to work with you on this project. These meetings are a terrific opportunity because you can introduce the speaker and get to be the star. You let the speaker fill the role of Shamu at SeaWorld. Shamu is what brings all the customers to SeaWorld, and then SeaWorld makes its money by selling food and merchandise to the people who come to the park. You use the speaker as a draw to bring people to you, and then you use the event as an opportunity to become known within the industry.

If you use your events as a membership recruitment opportunity for the association, you will get even more cooperation. Ask the association to invite non-members as well as members to the event and have some membership applications on-hand at the meeting. If you are able to sign up a new member or two (or more), try to get payment right then and there. Ask them to put it on their credit card or to give you a check on site. There is nothing more powerful than being able to send the association's meeting planner or executive director three or four completed membership applications that you were able to obtain on their behalf. This will garner a lot of cooperation in the future. Not to mention it will make you look good to everyone who attended the meeting. You will get to meet prospects, and probably some current customers, who will see you as an individual who cares about their industry—and them—building valuable relationships that will last. People want to buy things from people who make them feel good, and if you are that person who makes them feel good, you will win a lot of new business.

Associations are constantly looking for industry information that will be useful to their members. If you have a database of information, or if you are able to compile useful information through market research, it should be very well received by the association. The association will be eager to promote this information, and that can create profitable opportunities for you to get new customers.

Another technique is to create your own index or industry guide that you can publicize throughout an industry. Or you can create customer satisfaction surveys of individuals within an industry, similar to how J.D. Power creates its programs. J.D. Power creates surveys and provides recognition to companies that have reached a certain benchmark of quality within the survey. The recognition is nice, but if the company wants to use that recognition within its marketing, the company must pay J.D. Power a licensing fee. Whether or not you charge a licensing fee, publishing industry information is very useful to the industry's participants. It's another great way to forge a relationship with an association.

Solving a problem for an association is another way to promote your company. Trade associations often have difficulty getting the CEOs of their larger member companies to attend association events. Often these CEOs came in the past, and company owners of smaller members still attend, but the association is no longer drawing the CEOs of larger members. Over the years, these CEOs have gotten busy and spread thin, so they have decided to send members of their team to represent their company at events instead of attending themselves. So, here's the problem: You want to meet the CEO decision makers, and the association wants them to attend its meetings.

Here's a simple solution that thrusts you and your company into the spotlight and helps you to meet the exact people you are trying to reach. Offer to sponsor and, if necessary, facilitate a CEO forum for the association. The association invites CEOs only to a forum that is designed exclusively for them. You work with the association to develop an agenda and perhaps bring in a high-caliber speaker and/or facilitator. Through this forum, you get face time with the industry CEOs you've been trying to meet, and the association regains the participation of important members.

All these programs and opportunities help everyone involved in a number of ways. You, the vendor, benefit from increased market share. Here are some other benefits:

Lower acquisition and retention costs. Depending on your products or services and the way you use the association in your marketing, your costs to acquire new business will be lower. You will be focusing your message on a particular niche, so your message will be more relevant to and will gain greater attention from your target audience.

Image. Through participating in the association, you will increase your company's image within the industry or profession. You will be seen as an industry participant, as a supporter of those who are working to help the members succeed, and as one of those rare individuals who not only cares about the dollar, but also cares about the people involved. Such an image can increase your market penetration and provide additional revenue for you.

Cross sell. If you offer several different products and services, association events can provide opportunities for you to cross sell more products to the same people.

The associations also benefit for several reasons:

Membership value. The association's programs are evaluated by its members based on the extent they add value to the membership investment. Programs that address the needs of members are important for retaining members. Increasing the value of the association to its membership is critical to the association's long-time viability, and it is of primary concern to the association's leadership.

Association competition. Associations are constantly competing with all the other vendors that are working to get their members' dues dollars. If you will work with an association to create a unique program it can market to its members, that program will allow the association to differentiate itself in the marketplace for association membership dues.

Visibility. The programs and services you offer the association, in membership registration, newsletter content, and education content, all improve the visibility of the association itself. The more valuable and helpful content the association can provide, the better it will be viewed in the eyes of its current and potential members.

Want Your Endorsed Provider Program to Succeed? Make It Worth Their While!

Chip Kessler, owner of Extended Care Products Inc., has found the perfect partners to promote his money-saving programs and consulting services to nursing homes and assisted living facilities nationwide—the state health care associations.

"Our signature program is an educational DVD called *Setting Realistic Expectations* that nursing facilities can give to new admitting families," Chip says. "We offer the DVD through the state health care association at a pricing discount, and we work with the association in a revenue partnership program."

The DVD opens the door for Chip to promote his products and services, such as consulting, webinars, and seminars to help nursing facilities improve their marketing.

The revenue-sharing arrangement is a win-win. The associations have a membership benefit that produces revenue and new members, and Extended Care Products receives the implied endorsement of the associations.

And this program has withstood the test of time.

"We started this back in 2002," Chip says. "Now we've gotten into producing webinars and live seminars for state health care associations, where we pretty much do all the work. They promote the events to their members, and we do a 50/50 revenue split."

Chip converts webinar and seminar attendees into customers by promoting his website and offering time-limited discounts on his products and services.

Asked about the key to working with associations, Chip says it is important to design a relationship that is beneficial to the association.

"If associations don't think it's worth their while, they're not going to work with you," he says. "It's also important to obtain testimonials from your customers to help others feel comfortable about doing business with you. And finally, be persistent. When I started out, nobody knew who I was, so it was a matter of just keeping at it to build relationships. Once people came to trust us, they wanted to do business with us."

THE STRAIGHT FACTS ABOUT THE VALUE OF AN ASSOCIATION'S ENDORSEMENT

There's an ultimate test of physical endurance and mental fortitude: a six-day, 153.2-mile ultra marathon across the Sahara desert called the Marathon des Sables (Marathon of the Sands). Competitors carry their own supplies as they compete in temperatures exceeding 120 degrees. The longest one-day distance covers 50.6 miles and includes 14.3 miles of sand dunes.

Four-time champion Mohamad Ahansal grew up in the Sahara. And in a place where most just try to survive, the skills Mohamad learned helped him become a winner in one of the most grueling footraces in the world. Since 1997, either Mohamad or his older brother, Lahcen, had won the race, until 2011, when Rachid el Morabity, their trainee, beat Mohamad by seven minutes.

Morabity attributes his winning time to using a unique zigzag method to climb the large sand dunes that make up many miles of the race.

"Other runners, they go directly up the hill," Morabity says. "They don't notice the secret."

Even though it's easy enough to see the secret, instead of emulating the champion, competitors innovate their own "improvements" by trying to barrel directly up the hill. Their intuition tells them that a straight line is the shortest distance and the shortest distance is always the quickest. Instead of learning from the proven results of the winner, they follow their less experienced intuition.

I used to think the same way. I'd learn a technique or a strategy, and then I'd put my own spin on it. I'd say to myself, "That may have worked for him, but I'm going to improve it and make it work even better for myself."

It took me years to figure out the technique was already improved. There was no need for me to create my own innovations. Instead, I needed to get better at emulating what had already been proven to work.

I see people (who should know better) make this same mistake all the time. Instead of simply emulating what works, they try to make improvements. Or worse yet, they ignore the aspects that work and imitate the insignificant details.

They see, but they do not learn.

On its surface, working with an association may appear difficult. It may seem like the harder way.

However, it's similar to the Marathon des Sables champion's "shortcut" of zigzagging back and forth while climbing sandy dues for 13 miles. At first glance the zigzagging appears to add more distance. Why would you want to add steps when you are already running 50 miles through a desert?

It's because when you are running 50 miles, adding a few feet through slogging sand in an uphill climb saves you a lot of energy. That saved energy helps you endure longer and reach the finish line more quickly.

Although the results are clearly visible, marketers often do not learn. If you are ready to learn, here are the secrets.

An endorsed provider relationship is another way you can work with associations to produce membership benefit programs. If you have worked with an association to build a relationship, have worked with its members, and have created valuable content, it should be fairly easy for you to have an endorsed provider relationship with that association.

Within an endorsed provider relationship, the association becomes an active marketer of your products and services. The association markets your products and services to non-members as a benefit for joining the association, and it markets them to current members to drive up market share and participation.

For its efforts, the association will expect to receive a royalty for promoting your products and services. Any of the other programs already discussed in this manual could be marketed through an endorsed provider relationship.

Of course, you can produce a great deal of content and gain plenty of notoriety for your business through an association without ever engaging in such a relationship, but doing so has its advantages. Some of the benefits of using endorsed provider relationships include better recognition within an industry, active participation of the association's staff in promoting your products and services, the distinction of being the chosen vendor by the association's leadership, the association's seal of approval on your products and services, the opportunity to put "association chosen vendor" and other recognition within your marketing materials, and the opportunity to send out direct mail and other telemarketing with a letter of endorsement or an audio endorsement from the association's executive director, elected president, or other appropriate leader.

All of this can provide valuable opportunities for the marketer, and in many cases an endorsed provider relationship proves to be very lucrative for everyone involved. However, there are some significant drawbacks and challenges to obtaining the endorsed provider status.

The process to become an endorsed provider is often treacherous and lengthy. I encourage anyone who wants to work with an association to start simply and do traditional association marketing for an extended period of time before even considering an association endorsed relationship. Because associations are risk averse and busy, their first inclination will be to find reasons why such a relationship will not work. Plus, they will be even more reluctant to enter into an endorsed provider relationship with outsiders they do not really know.

As a vendor, you can get immediate access to an association's membership by registering to attend an event, submitting an article for the newsletter, or exhibiting at a trade show. An endorsed provider relationship can take a lot longer to establish. It can easily take a year to build the relationship, and during that time, you will have lost out on countless other opportunities to get your marketing message to members and to generate new customers.

Endorsed relationships are best done after you already have an established relationship with the niche and you can easily see how the association's additional labor and marketing support for your product will create new sales.

When structuring endorsed provider relationships, generally a royalty is paid based on sales volume. This can be in addition to other fees or cost considerations, but generally the arrangement involves some sort of percentage of business volume. This is good for the vendor because the costs will often scale as the revenue increases, making it inexpensive to start this process and only costing you more as your sales volume increases. But it also provides very little incentive for the association if the endorsed relationship is not immediately successful.

For companies considering endorsed provider relationships, the primary benefit of the association's sponsorship is increased sales efficiency, that is, more sales for each promotion investment dollar. The association's sponsorship gives the vendor enhanced credibility and recognition within the marketplace. Companies gain additional sales by tapping into the members' loyalty to their association and the association's credibility with its members.

A direct mail promotion using the association's logo may be more noticed and read by the association's members. Individuals receiving sales materials are often very resistant and skeptical about sales pitches. However, this can be greatly reduced by the association's stamp of approval through an endorsed provider relationship. The higher response rates and sales results of these promotions may readily overcome the increased costs of any profit-sharing arrangements.

An association's membership provides a unique marketing opportunity for companies. Because associations are formed around niche groups, these demographics can be used to tailor the marketing methods to the target audience. Endorsed providers are able to avoid the difficult and essential process of establishing themselves as a provider within a marketplace. Receiving the endorsement of an association also serves to differentiate the company's products or services from its competition's. Many of the endorsed provider relationships are offered on an exclusivity basis, which can prevent competitors from participating in the association's meetings, trade shows, and other events.

An endorsed provider relationship gives the company a license to use the association's name and logo on the marketing materials directed toward the association's membership. This can improve the effectiveness of both sales and marketing. Association members are generally more eager to open mail that comes from the association to which they have paid dues to belong. In essence they have paid to receive that mail. Thus, they are much more likely to open and read mail from their association than they are from a vendor they have not heard of before. Also, if the member knows the association has reviewed the vendor's background, has verified references, and understands the offer is a benefit to the member, there is much less sales resistance for the buyer considering the product. Marketers working within an endorsed provider relationship also find that association members tend to spend more money. The cost of sale is lower, and the average sale is higher. Member loyalty is demonstrated by the fact that associations experience high renewal rates. This established link between members and their association generates value for the endorsed marketer. Potential for long-term profits from loyal customers increases the attractiveness of an endorsed provider relationship.

As an endorsed provider, you might choose to offer an education program the association would not otherwise have for its members. Or you might provide books or other publications or a subscription the association could help market. Because associations are interested in improving membership benefits and improving their non-dues revenue programs, they are often very receptive to these sorts of activities.

Typically within an endorsed provider relationship, the association is very content with 1 percent of an insurance program or a fraction of a percent on a rental car or a shipping program. So, if you are able to come to the association with a 20-80 or 30-70 or 40-60 arrangement where you get the majority of the income but the association does benefit financially from its participation, your offer should be well received. On its side of the bargain, the association will typically provide you with endorsed mailings to its membership. These can be mailings the association sends on your behalf in the association's envelopes with a letter on the association's letterhead directed to members that explains the value of your products or services and the reasons the members need to purchase them for their benefit.

Associations will also provide free newsletter advertising for vendors to help promote their endorsed products or services. Associations often need to fill several pages in the newsletter, and your ad is as good as an article in their eyes. As the vendor, you will usually be expected to provide the artwork for your ad, which the association managers will be happy to run as part of the endorsed provider relationship you have with the association.

Editorial Content
Associations are always looking for good content for their newsletters. As part of the endorsed provider relationship, the association will be happy to run a series of articles, perhaps a monthly article featuring you and the problems you can solve for members. After all, because of the relationship, the more the association's members buy your products and services, the more the association makes in the bargain. Association managers are often very eager to allow you to fill their newsletters with potential revenue-producing content.

Exhibit Space
Endorsed provider relationships often include stipulations that the vendor will exhibit at the association's meetings. Whether or not there is a booth fee for that exhibit is one of the good points of negotiation between the vendor and the association.

Fulfillment

Many associations will even take over the roles of
accepting orders and filling and shipping products on
behalf of a vendor. Typically only larger associations will
do this, and of course the royalty payments will have to
justify the additional service level. But very often you
will be able to achieve a turnkey relationship with an
association.

Special Programs or Meetings

You will often be able to negotiate with the association
to include you as a speaker at each of its meetings or at a
certain number of meetings per year. This can be a good
opportunity to get face time with members to promote
your endorsed products and services.

The Responsibilities of an Association Promoting an Endorsed Provider Relationship

When entering into an endorsed provider relationship,
the association agrees to endorse the products or services
being offered by the vendor. The association agrees to
allow its logo to be used on all promotional materials,
including brochures and envelopes, letterhead, flyers, and
advertisements. In addition, these announcements may
be run in association magazines, email broadcasts, and
periodicals.

When endorsing a provider, associations will usually
identify a staff person to serve as the primary point of
contact for both the vendor and the members. This
staff person serves as a liaison, reviewing and approving
the use of the association's name and logo and seeking
members' and committees' approval as appropriate for

the main marketing plan. Once the marketing programs are launched, the responsibilities include monitoring performance, executing on the association's responsibilities for the marketing effort, and coordinating with everyone to ensure the membership's satisfaction.

The Responsibilities of a Company Offering an Endorsed Provider Relationship

First and foremost, the company seeking an endorsed provider relationship is responsible for creating and delivering high-quality products or services. The marketer usually pays the costs and handles the logistics of administering, operating, and promoting the marketing program. This includes development of marketing materials, executing the marketing plan, providing customer service, providing account service, tracking sales, and paying royalties due to the association.

The costs of promotion include graphic design, printing materials, copy writing, postage, mailing, and telemarketing. Generally any promotions that include the association's name or logo will need to be approved by the association before they can be printed and mailed. The association has a good legal reason for this approval process: to protect the style and quality of its trademarks.

In addition, the marketer should create a detailed marketing plan.

Direct Mail

Although many associations are switching away from direct mail because of its perceived cost, for some associations, direct mail is an excellent communication and marketing tool. For those associations that use direct mail, they use it to promote their membership opportunities, to promote their education programs, and to recruit vendors and sponsors for their meetings. They use direct mail because it is proactive, cost effective, and can be targeted exactly to the prospects that need to receive the message.

Within most endorsed provider relationships, direct mailings to the association's members and potential members are the primary means of promotion. Brochures, sales letters, catalogs, and other materials may also be mailed to members by the endorsed company using the association's logo.

Email

Another method of promoting an endorsed provider relationship is by email broadcasting. These will look like the same email blasts that go out to announce a legislative program or member news, but they will also include information about the endorsed provider's products and services being offered to members. Email broadcasts are excellent because they are inexpensive and can be tailored with specific demographic criteria in mind.

Telemarketing

Calling an association's members to promote an endorsed provider relationship can generate terrific results. However, most associations are concerned about the negative repercussions of allowing vendors to call their members on the association's behalf. They are concerned that the vendor's intrusion on their members' time (with the association's endorsement) might cause members to lose interest in participating in the association.

Still, telemarketing does have some advantages over other promotional vehicles. The obvious advantage is speed. The telemarketing program can notify all the members of the opportunity within a number of weeks whereas a direct mail campaign can take several months. With a telemarketing program, the endorsed vendor has the opportunity to get direct feedback on the viability of the offer and can gauge members' as well as nonmembers' interest in the products or services. If you find an offer is particularly successful during the first 1,000 calls, you may find that experience is consistent with the rest of the list. Conversely, if you have not made any sales in the first 1,000 calls, then you may want to evaluate the viability of continuing to market the offer.

Advertising

Often associations have advertising vehicles available within publications, websites, and events. These can include ads within a membership magazine, on a website, or in a conference program. I've often heard from marketers that these advertising vehicles don't provide an adequate return on investment. I won't argue with that. If you run an ad with a tracking mechanism, you'll probably find that the ad, by itself, doesn't generate sufficient leads to justify the investment. However, ads can be a powerful awareness strategy. Although the member reading the association's magazine won't always pick up the phone and call you in response to an advertisement, that member may very well be more receptive to your phone call when he or she remembers seeing your ad.

Your association partner should want to offer advertising as part of your endorsed relationship to help you get the word out about your products and services. Ads in the association's publications provide a great way to become the dominant provider within your industry. Oftentimes you can negotiate exclusivity if the deal is going to provide sufficient revenue to the association to offset any advertising revenue it might lose from competing advertisers. Either way, advertising can be a powerful addition to your endorsed provider relationship.

Press Releases

Associations send out frequent press releases and often include information about a new membership program or an endorsed provider's products and services. This can be another resource for you to gain improved visibility with members.

Turning a Relationship Into a Member Benefit

Dr. Joey Faucette is a business consultant who helps people learn to "Work Positive in a Negative World." Joey has used his relationships with associations to promote his services for several years.

To get started, Joey chose an industry where he had some experience: newspapers, and the free ones in particular.

"These are your community needs papers that don't charge anything," Joey explains. "You might know them as *Shoppers*, *American Classified*, or *Thrifty Nickel*."

Joey gathered information on the free papers and the associations they join and found that more than half of the 7,000 free papers across the country belong to publishers associations. He set about building relationships within the industry by offering to speak at association events and offering free content for association newsletters.

Now he offers a 50 percent commission to associations that promote his *Seven Weeks to Work Positive* program. And responding to the trend of printed papers converting to digital, Joey has created a streaming internet radio show that helps free papers diversify their income by offering audio ads to customers.

"Basically our customers upload the information they take in for display ads into a system, and we produce the audio ads," Joey explains. "It's easy for them to do, and with very cost-effective prices for their clients, these free papers are able to generate six figures of income."

As Joey learns more about his customers' problems, he adds to his products and services, tailoring what he does to meet the needs of the market. For example, he sells his books to be used as client appreciation gifts, cosponsors Work Positive events with newspapers and chambers of commerce, and continues to expand his reach by providing content for new groups across the country.

How to Go From Pest to Welcome Guest With Associations

I played my best golf during college. On Tuesdays and Thursdays, my last class of the day was Governmental Accounting. I'd look over at my friend and with one nod to each other, we knew—there was no way we could sit through a lecture when it was so nice outside. So, we'd get up and leave for the golf course before class started.

Even when I was playing my best, I was a hack. I was self-taught, "gripping and ripping." Don't get me wrong, I practiced. I'd go out on the driving range and hit balls. Or we'd practice on the putting green by betting each other a dollar per hole for whoever sank a putt with fewer strokes.

But when it was time to drive the ball, I'd stand on the tee box, take a swing, and see how far it went. I had no idea how professional golfers planned their shots; I'd never had a coach. I was trying to learn on my own.

What I learned later in life is that the professional's approach is completely different. And although it made complete sense when it was explained to me, I doubt it would have ever occurred to me on my own.

Golfers begin every hole with a careful analysis. First they examine where the hole is and decide on which side of the hole they want their ball to land on the green. Based on that, they decide from where they want to make their approach shot. This tells them where they want their ball to land on the fairway when they hit their drive shot.

They start each hole with an outlined, step-by-step plan. Then they can make adjustments along the way to minimize the steps they must take.

Unfortunately, few business owners take this same approach. They act the way I did when I was learning to play golf—just grabbing a club and swinging it as hard as I could.

Too many beginning marketers just grab a tactic and swing as hard as they can. They start with the tool and try to use it to its fullest, without having any idea what they want that tool to do for them.

This is the most important insight in this book. I'm revealing the "secret sauce" that makes my efforts to create endorsed provider programs so successful. Instead of offering the association a program that is a mere money maker, you offer a program that is a money maker *and* a new member recruitment tool for the association.

Associations are actively searching for products and services that will generate more members for their organizations. Sure, retaining their current members is important, but those stubborn folks who haven't yet joined the organization are more frustrating to association managers.

If you position your products or services as a membership benefit and design a membership recruitment mailing for your association partners, they will be extremely motivated to promote you and your services to their entire list of potential members.

Step 1: Create a membership benefit program associations can implement to improve membership recruitment and retention

One of the easiest benefit offerings is one I mentioned in an earlier section of this manual, the "Expert-on-Call." The Florida Movers and Warehousemen's Association has paid a fee to Seay Management Consultants every month for 20 years so that Seay Management's staff of labor law experts will take members' calls and answer questions. Of course, these questions provide Seay Management the opportunity to sell its services. "Oh, so you are having trouble with a wage and hour investigation. Would you like to have a professional represent you during those negotiations?"

But what is more important to the association is that this program gives the Florida Movers and Warehousemen's Association the opportunity to sell access to an "on-call labor consultant" as one more benefit for joining the association. Since all movers have labor problems, this is a compelling reason to join.

It is helpful if you can create a small level of service that can be sold or given to an association so it can add an item to its membership benefit offerings. Can you provide the association with a monthly newsletter article, special reports, a member tele-training program, or other service? These will encourage the association to promote you and your services and drive their members to you as the "industry expert."

Step 2: Develop an up-front bonus item an association can produce and deliver to each of its members

If you are a publisher, you can design a membership benefit around your monthly newsletters, a product based on your monthly interviews, or a special report. These can be licensed to an association to use as a premium for joining the association. Or you can offer a price discount to association members for your products. Either way, you will encourage the association to use your materials and to promote you in their marketing materials directed toward their membership prospects. This will be a very powerful endorsement of you and your expertise.

Step 3: Develop a list of ideas, sales letters, and do-it-for-you resources to train associations how to leverage the value from your benefit offering

Any time you provide a benefit to an association, you are going to have to develop the sales materials and vendor resources necessary to maximize the association's marketing efforts. Make sure you provide the association with sales copy, graphics, and materials that are ready to use to make you look good. Generally association managers can find time to send information to their members; however, they won't always be adept at creating effective marketing.

You will need to provide information for the association's website, complete with links to your site for more information. Plus, you will need to provide all the marketing materials for email, mail, and newsletter promotion of your new membership benefit offering.

Step 4: Determine how to make your membership benefit program free to the association through sponsorship, new member revenue, product sales commissions, or a special conference

It is fine to ask an association to pay you for providing an additional membership benefit to its members. After all, you are helping the association to sell memberships and generate revenue.

However, the money the association is paying you has to come out of an expense line item. That line item was created without designating money to pay you. If there is any way you can help fund that line item through a third party sponsorship, you will get the money you want while making it easier for an association to offer your products to its members.

Work with individuals and companies that are already sponsoring the association's events and programs. Contact them to ask if they are interested in co-branding a new membership benefit for the association's membership. They can pay a small fee for recognition as a provider of the program. Meanwhile, you not only get the credibility of the association's endorsement, but also the endorsement of your sponsor partner. This is a very powerful combination, both from the standpoint of getting the association to agree to promote your program and from the perception of value on the part of the members.

Step 5: Create marketing materials for the association to include in its new member welcome kits to notify new members about your program

Using your marketing materials, the association will be able to promote your membership benefit offering to its newest association members. If your offer is designed to be ongoing, it will be extremely beneficial to provide a report or two to the association to distribute to its newest members. If nothing else, supply the association with a public domain book for which you have written a foreword and have listed yourself as the sponsor on the cover.

Step 6: Create a membership marketing sequence associations can use to recruit members based on the value delivered by your program

Finally, the real power. Create a marketing sequence an association can use to sell memberships by featuring your membership benefit program.

You can adapt your existing marketing materials. By adding some of the association's membership benefits and then editing the call to action to join the association, you will have created an effective membership marketing letter for the association to distribute to its potential members. Wouldn't it be powerful to have the associations in your target industries sending out your sales letters to promote you and your expertise?

Begin your association marketing efforts with careful thought about how your product or service can become a membership benefit for the association you are approaching. Then use the step-by-step approach to become a trusted resource so you can present your benefit and help the association recruit members and grow.

Why Is It So Hard to Get a Decision? (How to skip straight to the finish line)

"This is more work than I expected," a client told me.

What?!? More work than you expected? The association marketing program teaches you how to create a million-dollar-a-year marketing shortcut for business. Don't you think it should take some work?

I can still clearly remember praying to God, saying, "I don't care how hard I've got to work; just give me an opportunity to succeed." God answered my prayers, but there was no six-week program. It took me several years to figure it all out.

Building a new marketing system with associations takes work. I'm creating a brand new product in a brand new niche myself, and I sometimes catch myself saying, "Wow, I didn't realize it would take this much work." But then I realize that I'm doing work that's a lot easier than real work like marketing, planning, sales conversations, and follow-up.

Associations often receive unsolicited proposals from unheard-of providers with unknown track records, all seeking to have an endorsed provider status with the association. The association's staff is left with the task of determining which of these programs is worth pursuing. Here is a quick list of criteria association executives use when judging the value of a potential vendor:

1. **Understanding.** Does the proposal reflect a good understanding of this association's marketing capabilities, staffing, and motivation?

2. **Relevancy.** Is this proposal relevant to the members? There are a lot of generic programs offering generic discounts for common products and services. Something that is more specific and relevant to an association's membership is going to get a higher level of consideration than one that is generic and could be applicable to any association or group of people.

3. **Commitment.** Proposals are often judged by the resources the potential vendor has. Do the individuals marketing the products or services have the commitment and the sales force necessary to sell the program and generate the desired results?

Quite a few of the small or start-up companies that approach associations are really just generating new problems for the association and not creating solutions. When they pitch a program to the organization, they expect the association's endorsement to be a silver bullet that automatically sells goods and services. Unfortunately, that is not the case. An association's endorsement can be very valuable, and using the association's resources and communication media can be an effective method for the vendor to get the word out about his or her products or services. However, it is not the end of the road; it is simply the beginning of a very powerful strategy.

4. **Need.** Associations are looking for solutions to problems. If your proposal solves problems the membership is facing, you will get more attention than others will. If association members are facing a crisis within their industry or are having considerable trouble with particular issues, proposals that clearly address those problems and offer solutions to those concerns are going to get more consideration than ones that do not.

5. **Value.** Does the proposal offer members a real value? Too often a proposal simply emphasizes the non-dues income it will generate and ignores the benefits for members. If a program is not going to generate additional justification for membership dues, most associations will not engage in that program, even if there is some promise of non-dues revenue. The program must clearly be something that is not otherwise available to the members and offered at a price that is not available to non-members.

6. **Membership magnet.** Are the products or services being offered by the vendor something that will attract more membership dues to the association? If so, those offers are going to be considered before any others. The first concern of every association executive is tracking the number of members in the organization. As membership increases, so does the prestige and value

of the association. Vendors who offer programs that will bring more members and membership dues to the association will have a very good opportunity for success. Not only because of the potential to collect more dues, but also because the association executive will be afraid you will take the program away from his or her organization and offer it to a competing association.

7. **Non-dues revenue.** Finally (and perhaps, surprisingly, least important), will the proposal provide more money for the association's other programs? A couple of years ago, associations were ready and willing to engage in any non-dues revenue program that came around. Now they are more selective about the programs they endorse. First, association managers are looking for programs that will not hurt them or their association. Second, they are looking for programs that will attract members to the association. Third, they are interested in making sure the program will provide non-dues revenue for the association. So, non-dues income is an important issue to bring up when you are marketing a program to an association; however, it is no longer the top priority for an association manager.

Most likely, any trading of money will require approval from the board of directors. Very few vendors ever contact the board directly; instead they are content to allow the staff to attend the board meeting and make the pitch.

When the executive agrees to take your offer to the board of directors, ask if he or she has any problem with you sending a few marketing materials to the board in advance of the meeting. You might say to the executive,

"You and I both know it is critical that your board members trust me before they are going to agree to enter into this relationship. Do you have any problem with me sending them a letter of introduction and information in advance of the meeting? Of course, this is the first hurdle we'll both need to pass before the program we created together will be a successful revenue generator for your association."

Once the executive has agreed and has given you the contact list, create and implement a marketing plan targeted to that board roster.

The way group dynamics work, if any one of the board members raises an objection, it is likely the others won't be brave enough to counter it. You might think you could count the number of board members, identify if you have support from a majority, and then rest easy knowing your agreement will be approved. However, almost everything is unanimously approved or rejected. If anyone is adamantly against a particular proposal, most likely it will be rejected.

Although the staff members may be convinced your proposal is good for the association, it is unlikely they will risk their own necks to vigorously help your proposal get ratified by their board.

Staff Obstruction
The most common obstacles to getting your proposals approved by the association are the roadblocks created by staff.

Here is an example: I have been trading emails with a content provider who wants to be a speaker at my annual meeting. He has been extremely diligent and persistent.

But unfortunately, in his case, he has not gotten past the staff obstacle. I gave the guy a chance to speak a few years ago, and he did a poor job. I'm not going to give him another chance to disappoint my members. My members depend on me to provide informative content with speakers who are entertaining. This guy was neither informative nor entertaining. He's a nice guy, but he will never get on my stage again. With that glimpse into how an association executive's mind works, let me give you a few more tips so you can be successful when working with an association's staff.

As I have mentioned before, an association's staff members are very fearful, they are very overworked, and they are usually very frustrated with their board of directors. However, many times when a member comes to me with a proposal for an education program, I am practically obligated to put it on the program. If that member is going to come to the event or send employees, and he or she has told me, "Hey, this is something that is important to me. I would like for you to include it in the next meeting program," it is terribly difficult for me to ignore that request. Therefore, if you have an opportunity to ask a member to contact an association staff person on your behalf to promote a course offering, I suggest you try to do it.

Here's another strategy you can use even when you haven't been successful in getting on the education program or if the staff has been unwilling to cooperate with an endorsed provider agreement. Instead of focusing on your ideas, reach out to ask what the staff needs.

Maybe what the staff members need right now is a news article, or perhaps they need some press help. Perhaps they need some industry statistics, and a speaker at their meeting is not what they are looking for. The staff person you reached may be so busy trying to create content for the newsletter that he or she cannot focus and give your request to present at the annual meeting the attention it deserves. So instead, solve that staff person's problem with the newsletter content, and he or she will be much more interested in helping you get on the program.

You can also work around the staff by contacting the elected leaders of the association and working through them to gain access to the organization. The president and other executive officers often have broad authority to make suggestions for programming and newsletter articles. This can be another opportunity. Certainly the association's staff members may be upset or frustrated by you going around them, but if they have been uncooperative, then you have little choice. Ordinarily the association's leaders are hurried because not only do they have association matters to address, but they also have their own business responsibilities. In essence, they have two jobs, so they may not be able to be helpful in every case. But it is certainly worth a shot to contact the association's president, or perhaps the past president, the vice president, or the president-elect. It is a good opportunity to speak with a prospective client about something that is not about you and your business; it is about the association. It is something they are obviously interested in since they spend so much time volunteering. So, you have an opportunity to build a relationship with two or three people, and who knows, it could result in your being included in the annual meeting, the newsletter, or something else you are seeking to do with the association. I strongly encourage you to contact the association's elected leaders to build relationships with them as well as with the association's staff.

Identifying and Targeting Associations

The key to successful association prospecting is to know everything you can about the association: its membership, the budget, the staff members, its desire to attract members, and the need for non-dues income. Some of this information is readily available, but most will require a good deal of research and a careful review of the association's website(s). The success of your marketing campaign will hinge largely on the relevancy of your message to your audience. The more information you are able to obtain, the more relevant a message you will be able to create.

Internet Search

Although it's obvious once I mention it, I'm amazed by how few marketers think to start their search for associations on Google. Just type the name of your industry followed by the word "association" to identify potential associations with which you can work.

National Directories of Affiliates

While your first inclination might be to go for the "big boy" national association, you may have better opportunities to start your efforts with state and local associations. In almost any industry, you will find many members who are active in their state and local associations but never attend national association events. Plus, you may find state and local associations more willing to work with you because they are smaller and less bureaucratic than large national associations.

You'll often find directories of state and local associations on the national association's website. In an effort to serve their members by providing information, national associations often list the contact information for their affiliates throughout the country. This can be a huge shortcut for marketers like you who are looking for associations with which to work.

Association Directories

Many tools are available to expedite your research, including directories, databases, and direct mail lists. Using these tools, you can identify several associations that have the programs that will provide the most benefit to you and your marketing efforts.

Association directories differ in their exact content and profile information. Most will contain:

- Association's name
- Telephone and fax numbers
- Organization's purpose
- Membership size
- Staff size

- Address
- Executive's name and title
- Historical background
- Annual budget
- Publications and conventions information

When contemplating a directory to use, it is important to consider how the information is indexed. Most of the time you will not be looking up a specific association but seeking information regarding associations that serve a particular industry or profession. While most directories are indexed alphabetically by association names, others are also indexed by industry, occupation, budget, location, and even association acronyms. Each index will save you time and will help to streamline your prospecting efforts.

The American Society of Association Executives offers an online directory of associations that are members of its association called the "Gateway to Associations." By entering a key word (e.g., truck) in the "Association name contains" field, you can generate a list of every member association that deals with that industry or subject. You can narrow your search by filling in the location fields.

http://www.asaecenter.org/Community/Directories/
associationsearch.cfm
American Society of Association Executives
The ASAE Building
1575 I Street N.W.
Washington, DC 20005-1103
Phone: 888-950-2723; 202-371-0940 (in Washington, D.C.)
Fax: 202-371-8315

By joining the ASAE, you can obtain access to its members' only directory with contact information for members available at http://collaborate.asaecenter.org/ Home.

Although the ASAE doesn't publish email addresses, it does provide a way to send a message to members and provides telephone numbers for follow-up calls.

The following directories have cross reference guides sorted by industry and profession. You can go to the niche you are trying to reach and find a cross reference to all the organizations within that niche.

Encyclopedia of Associations, Gale Research Company, Cengage Learning, 10650 Toebben Drive, Independence, KY 41051. Features more than 100,000 associations for $505.00. Generally considered the leader in listing trade associations. National and state/regional organizations are broken into two volumes.

Associations Yellow Book, Leadership Directories, 104 Fifth Avenue, New York, NY 10011; 212-627-4140. An online directory of more than 1,000 national trade and professional associations for $445.00 per year. http://www. leadershipdirectories.com

National Trade and Professional Associations of the United States, Columbia Books, 8120 Woodmont Avenue, Suite 110, Bethesda, MD 20814; 202-464-1662. Features 7,800 associations for $299.00. *State & Regional Associations of the United States* ($199.00). http://www. columbiabooks.com

AssociationExecs.com, the team behind the *National Trade and Professional Associations of the United States*, publishes a website for online access to its database of associations. Subscriptions begin at $799.00 a year. http://www.associationexecs.com/

In addition to these resources, here are a few free directories that may be helpful to your research:

WEDDLE's Association Directory, http://www.weddles.com/associations/index.cfm

Info Please Directory of U.S. Societies & Associations, http://www.infoplease.com/ipa/A0004878.html

Wikipedia List of industry trade groups in the United States, http://en.wikipedia.org/wiki/List_of_industry_trade_groups_in_the_United_States

Who Else Is Selling to Associations, and How Are They Doing It?

I get frustrated when I hear about the social structure in high school. But then I realize it can be the same way everywhere else, if you let it.

My daughter, Samantha, has several classmates she has known for many years. They went to elementary and middle school together. But she doesn't talk to them. Confused, I asked her why.

She told me, "They are 'populars,' and I'm not. I hang out with the band." Definitions can be interesting. According to high school social vernacular, "populars" doesn't mean these students are well known or well liked; it means they are full of themselves. Samantha is looking for people who are more accepting of each other, and that's the band kids.

I don't like this because I want everyone to like my daughter, and I want her to be the most popular kid in the school. What is more important, I don't want her to limit her own choices and experiences by predetermining she's going to exclude people based on which group they are in. Yet I do the same thing.

In the late 1990s, I was well known in the association world. (The association world is made up of the people who run associations.) After I learned about info-marketing, I thought to myself, "Association people don't get it. I'm going to start hanging out in the marketing world, or more specifically, the Dan Kennedy world. I'm going to be part of Planet Dan." I shut myself out of a lot of experiences I could have had because of a false feeling of superiority.

Because we are so busy, we have to assign people to categories. In the end, all the categories are simply subcategories of these two: important and not important.

Certain people end up in the important category: spouse, kids, boss, and your clients. Others end up in the not important and can be ignored: pestering salesperson, the loser who keeps hanging around me at the office, and Kim Kardashian. Our customers do the same thing; they are making these judgments about us!

While this book shows you how to break down all the social structures to which association managers typically adhere, it's important to see how the association world is structured. It will give you an important insight into the social order.

Following are two examples of others you will likely encounter as you market to associations. Studying them and understanding their tactics will be useful to you. This way you can quickly identify the players and step right through to become one of the "populars" yourself.

Hotel sales representatives from around the country are contacting association executives trying to encourage them to book meetings at their hotels. Associations have meetings ranging from large conventions with multiple programs, to regional events, to one-day programs, to smaller board meetings and retreats. Venue providers of all sizes and types are contacting association executives asking them for the opportunity to host a meeting. The sheer volume of marketing calls, hotel advertising, and sales letter contacts is staggering. Many organizations get several such mailings or calls every day.

In addition to the hotels themselves, most destinations throughout the country are represented by convention and visitor bureaus. These organizations also make sales presentations to meeting planners and association executives, trying to encourage them to book any number of hotels within their area. These contacts are rarely instead of direct hotel contacts; generally they are in addition to the hotel contacts. So, the association executive will have the convention and visitor bureau for New York City calling as well as each of the convention hotels within New York City. The volume of contacts can be overwhelming.

It is useful to study the way hotel vendors choose to communicate with meeting planners and association executives. They talk about the features of the hotel, the beautiful pool, or the beautiful beaches. But rarely do they communicate the main benefit of booking an event at their hotel, which presumably would be the association would have more attendees at that venue than it would at any other venue it could choose.

Let's look at a second example:

Another group of sales calls comes from technology providers. If it is not a fax broadcast provider or a web programmer, it is a membership database provider trying to contact association executives. The association market is such a small world that it can be reached pretty efficiently through a telemarketing operation, and many of the technology providers have aggressive telemarketing programs to get the word out to association executives about their products and services.

The way these potential technology vendors interact with associations is very similar to the way I have suggested you interact. Not only do they do direct mail and telemarketing, but the smarter ones also participate as members in the associations of association executives. In addition to a national society, the American Society of Association Executives, there are state, regional, and even city associations throughout the country that represent association executives.

Technology vendors write articles for the associations' trade journals. They buy advertisements in those journals. They show up at events and exhibit at trade shows in addition to all their other marketing efforts.

From experience I can tell you that the vendors who participate in the associations' events do better with their telemarketing and direct mail than the vendors who do not. That is a powerful message for anyone trying to reach any market. For improved leverage of your current marketing dollars, you need to participate as a member of the association of the industry you are targeting, write articles for the trade journals, and participate in the industry's events.

DON'T GET TACKLED AT THE GOAL LINE
CRITICAL TAX CONCERNS YOU NEED TO ADDRESS THAT USUALLY SCARE ASSOCIATIONS AWAY FROM "STRANGERS" LIKE YOU

Associations are tax-exempt organizations, but they are subject to tax on income that is unrelated to their mission or business (unrelated business income tax or UBIT), which includes many forms of non-dues income. Associations may risk the loss of their entire tax-exempt status if they do not correctly report their non-dues revenue to the Internal Revenue Service.

While service development and generating non-dues income are huge priorities for associations, the vendors courting them with those opportunities must understand the impact IRS regulations have on an association's activities. Because associations are tax-exempt organizations as approved by the Internal Revenue Service, their activities are severely limited. Associations and professional societies generally fall into two of 23 tax-exempt categories. They are usually categorized as either 501(c)(6) or 501(c)(3).

Professional and trade associations are generally 501(c)(6) organizations while organizations representing individuals are generally 501(c)(3) organizations. 501(c)(3) organizations are a lot more limited in what they can do. They are limited in the political activities they can undertake, and they are completely forbidden to participate in campaigns for political offices. They do, however, have certain advantages. For example, 501(c)(3) organizations often qualify for special nonprofit postage rates since their activities are generally educational, and the donations given to 501(c)(3) organizations are tax deductible by the donor. In addition, 501(c)(3) organizations are often exempt from state and local taxes.

Most associations representing trades and professions are 501(c)(6) organizations. While these organizations are not restricted in their activities to influence legislation and political campaigns, they do not get the benefits of the tax deductibility of contributions made to them or the reduced postage rates. And these organizations are still subject to tax in situations where the group's income is outside of the association's tax-exempt purpose. The IRS considers many of the activities that an association carries out to promote an endorsed provider's products or services to be unrelated business income. These include the rental of lists, the sending of mailings, and other activities involved to promote the endorsed provider.

For instance, if the association creates an endorsed provider relationship with an insurance company where the insurance company pays the association a fee for all the policies entered into by the association's members, that revenue would probably be considered unrelated business income and would be taxable to the association.

One of the tax-exempt avenues open to an association is a royalty payment. Royalties are not considered to be unrelated business income. Royalty fees from the use of an association's name are provided a special exemption from UBIT, along with other passive income such as dividends and interest. The exemption dictates how the endorsed provider relationship agreement must be constructed and implemented between the marketer and the association. It is advisable for the association and the endorsed provider to work with legal counsel to design a contract that meets those requirements.

In general, a key distinction for characterizing revenue from an endorsed provider relationship for tax purposes is whether the association is an active participant or passive in the marketing. If the association is an active marketer of the program, some or all of the income will likely be viewed as unrelated to the tax-exempt purpose of the association. If, on the other hand, the association is only licensing its name, logo, and mailing list to the endorsed company and is not an active promoter of the marketer's program, the income is not subject to UBIT. For the income to be considered passive, the association cannot participate in a program's marketing activity. Active conduct such as providing free advertising, sending promotional letters from the association's officers, and inserting marketing materials into mailings to members can cause the IRS to consider the association's income derived from that activity to be subject to UBIT. If the association does become actively involved in promoting the endorsed provider's marketing programs, the association's expenses related to that advertising, marketing, or promotion may be used to offset the UBIT income so the tax is paid only on net revenue.

Associations cannot receive royalties in exchange for services they perform or for benefits they provide to the endorsed provider. In these situations, the association and the vendor must enter into two separate agreements. One agreement provides the association with royalties for the use of its name and its endorsement. A second agreement provides the association with fees for the services and benefits it provides the endorsed provider. This way the association is able to avoid taxes on the revenues it receives as royalties, and it pays taxes only on the payments for services it provides to the endorsed provider.

Most vendors who approach an association with a proposal for an endorsed provider relationship have no idea that this tax issue exists and are not at all interested in helping the association to mitigate taxes by creating the relationship in a tax-savings way. As a vendor who offers the association an endorsed provider relationship with the association's tax needs in mind, you will have a distinct advantage over everyone else trying to market this type of relationship.

Association Tax Considerations for Establishing Endorsed Provider Relationships

Here are some helpful tips for you to construct a marketing program within an endorsed provider relationship so the association can avoid unrelated business income tax:

1. The agreement for the program should be called a royalty agreement or a license agreement, and the payments should be called royalties.
2. To maintain passive involvement in the program, a contract should not require the association to assist the endorsed company in marketing its products or services.
3. The association may include provisions that require approval of the materials prior to distribution. This not only is allowed within the passive rules but is also important for the association to protect its trademark rights.
4. It is preferable to base the royalties on gross revenue.
5. The association should not share expenses for marketing the program with the endorsed provider, and the provider should pay fair market value for any advertisements in newsletters and magazines, as well as for exhibit space.
6. Avoid the term *agent* in the agreement. Neither party should be referred to as an agent of the other.
7. The agreement should affirmably state that there is no intent to create a joint venture or a partnership between the association and a provider.
8. All programs should always be referred to as the outside service provider's program and should not be the association's program.

CALL TO ACTION

Now you have all the tools you need to tap into the associations that are already serving your customers and prospective customers. Are you going to take advantage of this new opportunity?

Use the To-Do List below to write down your ideas on how you can reach out to the association market today.

TO DO LIST

- [ ]
- [ ]
- [ ]
- [ ]
- [ ]

From Reading to Collaboration

Most books are just another form of a lecture, with someone preaching away. However, this book is different. This book is a door to a new community of marketers who are curious about associations, who want to learn a better way to market, and who are willing to share shortcuts with each other.

You can join the community by sharing your questions and your stories with me. Visit www.YourAssociationShortcut.com to get on the newsletter list for updated resources, case studies, and success profiles.

I want to hear your comments about your frustrating situations and your big breakthroughs. You are welcome to reach out to me via email at RS@YourAssociationShortcut.com. You are also welcome to send me comments about this book along with any questions you have. I look forward to receiving your note.

Best wishes.

QUICK ASSOCIATION MARKETING PROGRAM IMPLEMENTATION

Although I'm extremely busy with my own businesses and my current coaching clients, I accept a limited number of new clients in cases where I believe the marketer has the tools to be a successful marketer to associations. All client relationships begin with a full-day fast implementation consultation.

Although it's considered a consultation *day*, it's really like a two-month consultation since we will use the month before we meet to prepare for our time together and the month after we meet to implement what we discussed during our session together. Many clients report the preparation is well worth their entire consultation investment.

After a month of preparation, we'll meet and create a plan together. I'll often provide resources and sometimes personal contacts to use to speed up your efforts.

For a full month after our consultation, I'll provide email support to answer questions as they come up. We will also have a one-on-one full hour consultation within a month after our time together so we can review how our plan has stood up to the real world, make course corrections as necessary, and review your detailed, step-by-step implementation plan.

If you'd like to schedule a complimentary 30-minute strategy call to discuss using association marketing for your business and to determine if marketing through associations is a good fit for you, contact Suzanne Hurst in my office at 850-222-6000 or via email at Suzanne@HelpMembers.com.